WordPress Websites in 2025

A Comprehensive Guide to Building Modern, High-Performing Websites with the Latest Features, Design Trends, and Best Practices

Chris Kirton

Table of Contents

Introduction 8

Chapter 1: Getting Started with WordPress 11

    1.1 Installing WordPress: Hosting and Domain Setup 15

    1.2 Exploring the WordPress Dashboard 18

    1.3 Essential Settings and Configurations 23

    1.4 Choosing and Installing a Theme 27

Chapter 2: Designing for 2025: Themes, Layouts, and Aesthetics........32

    2.1 Modern Design Trends in 2025 36

    2.2 Selecting the Right Theme for Your Website's Goals 41

    2.3 Creating an Impactful Layout..46

    2.4 Customizing Themes: Colors, Fonts, and Styles................50

Chapter 3: Creating Content That Engages and Converts 55

    3.1 Understanding Pages vs. Posts 59

    3.2 Building High-Impact Landing Pages.................................64

    3.3 Tips for Writing SEO-Optimized Blog Posts.......................69

    3.4 Multimedia Content: Images, Videos, and Interactive Elements 74

Chapter 4: Essential Plugins for a Powerful Website....................79

    4.1 Top WordPress Modules for 2025 84

    4.2 Security, Speed, and SEO Optimization Plugins................89

    4.3 E-commerce, Analytics, and Social Media Integration 93

    4.4 How to Install, Configure, and Manage Plugins................96

Chapter 5: Advanced Customization with Gutenberg and Page Builders 101

    5.1 Mastering the Gutenberg Editor..105

    5.2 Using Page Builders: Elementor, Divi, and More..............108

    5.3 Creating Dynamic and Responsive Content Blocks...........113

    5.4 Custom Code and Advanced Layouts 117

Chapter 6: Building an E-commerce Website with WooCommerce........122

    6.1 Setting Up WooCommerce for Online Sales......................127

    6.2 Product Management: Adding, Editing, and Organizing Products 132

    6.3 Payment Gateways, Shipping, and Taxes 137

    6.4 Managing Orders, Customers, and Reports.......................141

Chapter 7: Optimizing for Speed, Security, and Performance 147

7.1 Speed Optimization Techniques for 2025...151

7.2 Security Best Practices to Protect Your Website 156

7.3 Implementing Caching, CDN, and Lazy Loading...161

7.4 Monitoring Performance with Google Analytics and Site Tools 165

Chapter 8: SEO and Digital Marketing Strategies for WordPress 170

8.1 Keyword Research and On-Page SEO 174

8.2 Integrating Google Analytics and Search Console 178

8.3 Social Media and Content Marketing Tactics 183

8.4 Advanced Strategies: Schema Markup, Featured Snippets, and Core Web Vitals 187

Chapter 9: Accessibility and Compliance for WordPress Sites 192

9.1 Understanding Accessibility Standards (WCAG 2.1) 197

9.2 Making Your Website ADA Compliant 201

9.3 Tips for Inclusive Design and Usability..206

9.4 Tools for Testing and Improving Accessibility...210

Chapter 10: Maintaining, Scaling, and Updating Your Website.........................214

10.1 Regular Maintenance Tasks and Backups...217

10.2 Updating Themes, Plugins, and WordPress Core Safely 220

10.3 Tips for Scaling and Growing Your Site 223

10.4 Future-Proofing Your Website: Preparing for 2026 and Beyond.............227

Conclusion 232

Introduction

Welcome to Mastering WordPress Websites in 2025: A Comprehensive Guide to Building Modern, High-Performing Websites with the Latest Features, Design Trends, and Best Practices. Whether you're a business visionary, content designer, engineer, or somebody anxious to construct a strong internet-based presence, this guide will be your go-to asset for creating delightful, advanced WordPress sites.

In the present quick-moving computerized scene, a viable site is more than a straightforward web-based presence - it's a unique stage where organizations and people associate, rouse, and draw in with their crowds. With WordPress still at the front of web improvement, this stage offers unrivaled adaptability and power for amateurs and specialists the same. The catch? As the computerized world advances, so does WordPress. It is fundamental to stay aware of its most recent highlights, best practices, and arising configuration patterns to make your webpage hang out in a jam-packed web-based space.

Dominating WordPress Sites in 2025 demystifies WordPress for perusers at each expertise level. Beginning with the fundamentals, you'll figure out how to introduce WordPress, set up your site, and explore the dashboard like a master. From that point, we jump into the complexities of picking the right topics, building custom formats, and making a responsive, easy-to-use plan. On the off chance that you're prepared to take it up an indent, we'll investigate progressed subjects like Website optimization, webpage speed streamlining, web-based business incorporation, and module customization to transform your webpage into a high-performing force to be reckoned with.

This guide's obligation to the most recent improvements in WordPress makes it special. In 2025, WordPress will be more natural, adjustable, and strong than at any other time, coordinating historic devices and advancements like block-based altering, man-made intelligence-driven plan aides, and dynamic online business arrangements. This book keeps you at the forefront, telling you the best way to use these progressions to assemble sites that look perfect as well as convey results.

Every part gives noteworthy stages, genuine models, and experiences from fruitful WordPress experts. Whether you want to send off a business site, begin a blog, or make a mind-boggling web-based business stage, you'll find all that you want to rejuvenate your vision.

We should get everything rolling on dominating WordPress in 2025 - fabricating elite execution, in vogue sites that have an enduring effect.

Chapter 1: Getting Started with WordPress

Welcome to WordPress! Whether you intend to make a singular blog, a web business site, or a specialist portfolio, WordPress offers a remarkable stage to revive your vision. This part outfits you with the essential data expected to set up your most significant WordPress site, covering nuts and bolts from foundation to early customization. Ruling these underlying advances will set you on a course toward building major areas of strength for an attractive electronic presence.

Understanding WordPress: The Basics

WordPress is one of the world's most extensively used content organization structures (CMS), regarded for its convenience and flexibility. Initially arranged as distributing content to a blog stage, WordPress has formed into serious areas of strength for an instrument that maintains everything from essential locales to complex, incorporate-rich stages. This versatility makes it ideal for a large number of clients, whether they're fledglings researching the mechanized world or arranged planners managing high-traffic destinations. WordPress' wide library of modules and subjects considers expansive customization, engaging you to make a stand-out site fit to your cautious necessities and targets.

Choosing Between WordPress.com and WordPress.org

Before you hop into making your site, you'll need to pick between two transformations: WordPress.com and WordPress.org. While both arrangement solid site building limits, they diverge from respect to control and flexibility. WordPress.com is a worked-with stage that supervises most of the specific perspectives for you, including working with, updates, and fortifications. This game plan is perfect for clients searching for an immediate experience yet has confined options for customization except on the off chance that you climb to more elevated level plans. Of course, WordPress.org, generally called self-worked with WordPress, offers limitless power over your site, allowing you to change it energetically and present any modules or subjects you need. With WordPress.org, in any case, you'll need to manage the working with and upkeep. In this helper, we base on the versatility of WordPress.org, as it thinks about additional customization and control over your site's components and helpfulness.

Selecting a Domain Name and Hosting Provider

The space name and working with the provider you pick will be a fundamental part of the show and stamping of your site. Your space name is your page's area on the web, so select one that is fundamental, lines up with your page's inspiration, and mirrors your picture. Shoot for the stars and easy to spell, avoiding remarkable characters and numbers. At the point when your space is picked, this moment is the ideal open door to finding trustworthy working a provider. A good host will ensure your website moves ahead true to form and stacks quickly, two factors that are basic for client experience and web search device situating. Look for providers that offer high uptime, strong client help, security features, and versatile plans. Well-known choices integrate Bluehost, SiteGround, and WP Engine, each giving plans sensible to WordPress and various levels of traffic.

Installing WordPress: Step by Step

With a space and working with the provider, the resulting stage is to present WordPress. Many hosts offer "a solitary tick" foundation for WordPress, streamlining the game plan connection for juveniles. Simply sign in to your working with the account, find the WordPress installer, select your space, and fill in the crucial nuances, for instance, your site title and overseer certificates. In case your provider doesn't offer a solitary tick foundation, you can download WordPress from WordPress.org and genuinely move it to your server. At the point when the foundation is done, sign in to your WordPress dashboard, where you'll begin developing your site.

Exploring the WordPress Dashboard

The WordPress dashboard is your central control board for managing your site's substance, appearance, and settings. On the left-hand side, you'll find menus for making posts and pages, presenting points and modules, and tweaking your site's arrangement. Investigating the dashboard is principal, as it will be your fundamental mark of communication for making and managing your site. Posts are best for dynamic substance like blog articles, while pages are perfect for static substance, for instance, your About or Contact portions. This dashboard also gives you induction to modules, which license you to grow your site's convenience, and subjects, which control your site's arrangement.

Customizing Your WordPress Site's Appearance

At the point when your essential site is set up, this present time is the ideal open door to redo its appearance. WordPress offers a tremendous selection of subjects that choose the look and plan of your site. Inside the dashboard, investigate the Appearance fragment, where you can search for, present, and establish a subject that suits your vision. Many subjects offer innate customization decisions, allowing you to change tones, text styles, and plans with no coding data. Changing your subject to agree with your picture will work on your site's charm and help it lay out a huge association with visitors.

Launching Your WordPress Site

With your subject set up and beginning substance organized, you're ready to make your site live. Before shipping off, review your settings to ensure your site is smoothed out for execution, security, and client experience. Test your site's stacking pace and assurance it looks perfect on both workspace and mobile phones. Twofold truly investigates your security settings, presents an SSL underwriting, and considers completing a support reply to protect your data. When everything is all together, update your security settings to make your site uninhibitedly open, and your WordPress outing will officially begin.

This from the get-go part has outfitted you with the basics expected regardless of WordPress. In the going parts, we'll plunge into additional created strategies and frameworks for making a high-performing webpage that gets through and achieves your electronic targets.

1.1 Installing WordPress: Hosting and Domain Setup

To make a totally commonsense WordPress site, the underlying step is setting up a strong working with the provider and getting a striking space name. These focal parts are fundamental for your webpage's show, client experience, and online character. This section walks you through the essentials of picking a working provider, picking a space name, and acquiring WordPress to prepare your site.

Understanding Web Working with and Its Importance

Web working is the assistance that stores your webpage's data and makes it accessible on the web. Consider renting a modernized space where all of your records, pictures, and content are securely taken care of and open for visitors at whatever point. The idea of your working with a provider impacts your site's show, speed, uptime, and security. A reliable working provider is crucial to ensure that your webpage stays open to clients without impedances and loads quickly, the two of which are fundamental components for client responsibility and web crawler rankings. Working with providers contrasts in regards to execution, backing, assessing, and adaptability, so getting one that lines with your site's necessities is fundamental.

Picking the Right Kind of Working with

Web working comes in various types, each offering different levels of control, resources, and adaptability. The fundamental working with decisions consolidates shared working with, Virtual Classified Server

(VPS) working with, committed working with, and directed WordPress working with. Shared working is the most sensible decision and is perfect for tenderfoots, but it gives resources for various objections, which can impact execution during high-traffic periods. VPS working offers committed resources inside a typical environment, giving you favored control and execution over shared working. Committed working gives limitless oversight over a real server and is the best for greater, high-traffic objections. Regulated WordPress working with, arranged expressly for WordPress objections, manages WordPress-unequivocal enhancements, security, and updates, making it an eminent choice for clients who slant toward a hands-off approach.

Picking and Enrolling a Space Name

A space name is your web page's area on the web, giving clients a technique for getting to your page. While picking a space name, go all in, fundamental, and relevant to your picture or business. A strong space name should be easy to spell, expressive, and survey, helping clients find your site without any problem. Region names consistently end in developments like .com, .net, or .association, but new expansions, for instance, .blog or .shop offer extra checking decisions. At the point when you've picked a space name, you'll need to truly take a gander at its openness, as each area is extraordinary and can't be duplicated. Many working with providers offer space enrollment organizations, allowing you to purchase a region directly through them, now and again with bundled limits when gotten together with working with.

Setting Up Working with and Presenting WordPress

At the point when you have picked a working with provider and gotten your space, the accompanying stage is to set up your working with account and present WordPress. Most working providers have streamlined the WordPress foundation process, offering a "solitary tick present" feature for ease of use. Ensuing purchasing a working plan, you'll regularly be coordinated through a game plan cycle that consolidates picking the space for your site and planning major settings. Using the solitary tick present feature, track down the WordPress decision in your working with dashboard, pick your space, and follow the prompts to begin the foundation. During the cycle, you'll set up a chairman username and secret key, which you'll use to sign into your WordPress dashboard.

Planning Basic Settings for a Smooth Farewell

After WordPress is presented, stop briefly to plan several essential settings before shipping off your site. Access your WordPress dashboard by entering yourdomain.com/wp-manager and marking in with the capabilities you made. In any case, go to the Settings region and update your site's title, trademark, and time district to agree with your picture and region. Then, at that point, plan your permalinks, the URLs of your posts and pages, under the Permalinks settings. Picking a "Post name" structure is recommended for Web composition upgrades, as it makes great, clear URLs that will undoubtedly rank well in web crawlers. Finally, set up fundamental well-being endeavors by engaging SSL (Secure Connections Layer) expecting that your host offers it, which will encode data between your website and clients, further developing security and web search instrument situating.

Shipping off Your WordPress Site

With working with, space, and crucial settings set up, your WordPress site is good to go live. Lead a last overview to ensure your site stacks precisely and works immaculately across various devices. Test the speed, make sure that your SSL is dynamic, and assurance your URLs are suitably planned. These fundamental advances will clear a path for a consistent, high-performing WordPress site. By focusing strongly on this essential plan, you're establishing the groundwork for future turn of events, flexibility, and adaptability.

This hidden game plan is a surprising accomplishment, indicating the beginning of your journey into WordPress progression. In the approaching fragments, we'll examine how to make associating with content, re-try your page's arrangement, and impact modules to enhance your site's capacities and accomplishments.

1.2 Exploring the WordPress Dashboard

The WordPress dashboard fills in as the conflict space for managing your site. Here, you'll find everything expected to make content, change the site's appearance, and present modules that expand its helpfulness. Understanding the configuration and components of the WordPress dashboard will help you with surely investigating essential tasks as you develop and stay aware of your site. This fragment gives a broad manual for the WordPress dashboard, researching its essential parts and settings.

Getting to the WordPress Dashboard

After actually presenting WordPress, access your dashboard by going to yourdomain.com/wp-manager and entering the login affirmations made during foundation. Once endorsed, you'll be facilitated to the dashboard's presentation page, which gives a summary of your site's activity, including late posts, comments, and updates. This central place point similarly shows simple courses to routinely used instruments, furnishing you with an expedient framework of your site's status and any impending tasks.

Dashboard Diagram and Key Parts

The WordPress dashboard is parceled into two fundamental sections: the major workspace in the center and a menu bar on the left. The workspace locale revives effectively depending on what section you select from the menu bar. The left menu consolidates every principal ability, similar to Posts, Media, Pages, Comments, Appearances, Modules, Clients, Instruments, and Settings. All of these menu things are a way to additional significant features, allowing you to direct all that from content creation to state-of-the-art settings.

Posts and Pages: Administering Content

The Posts and Pages portions are where you'll make and manage your site's fundamental substance. Posts are ordinarily used for blog articles and other regularly revived content, facilitated successively. Pages, of course, are planned for static substance, similar to your About, Contact, and Organizations pages. Inside each fragment, you'll find decisions to add, modify, or eradicate content as well as arrange posts for better affiliation. In the boss, you can add text, pictures, and various media to build attractive pages and posts and save drafts as you work.

Media Library: Moving and Orchestrating Records

The Media region houses your site's photos, accounts, reports, and various media records. Here, you can move new reports, set up them, and supplement them into your posts or pages. The library's association point thinks about straightforward recording the board, giving decisions to add metadata, for instance, picture titles and alt text, which can additionally foster your webpage's Web composition improvement. By keeping media records facilitated, you ensure powerful access and a streamlined work process as your site creates.

Comments: Attracting with Your Group

In the Comments region, you'll supervise client correspondences on your posts. This locale shows all comments, where you can underwrite, reply, mark them as spam, or delete them. Attracting your group through comments manufactures neighborhood improves your substance. The Comments portion furthermore filters through spam using modules like Akismet, which can be engaged to reduce bothersome comments and keep a perfect, instinctive space for your perusers.

Appearance: Altering Your Site's Look and Feel

The Appearance fragment is where you'll change your web engineering's. Here, you can pick and change themes, supervise devices, and make menus. Picking a subject coordinates the visual style of your site while adjusting it licenses you to change nuances like tones, text styles, and configurations. Devices engage you to add parts like continuous posts, search bars, and virtual amusement interfaces with various bits of your site. Menus helps you with assembling site courses, making a more normal experience for visitors.

Modules: Extending Site Value

The Modules region is key for adding new components and functionalities to your WordPress site. Modules are pre-built instruments that grow what WordPress can oversee without requiring code data. From Web architecture improvement to online business features, modules offer solid decisions for redesigning your site. In this fragment, you can search for, present, activate, or deactivate modules, accommodating your site's capacity to resolve express issues.

Clients: Supervising Position and Assents

The Client's region grants you to manage who moves toward your WordPress site and controls their assets. WordPress plays worked in parts like Chief, Editor, Author, Ally, and Endorser, each with different levels of access. As the site owner, you can apportion occupations to partners, ensuring that endorsed clients can carry out immense upgrades or disperse content.

Instruments and Settings: Changing Your Site

The Instruments portion consolidates import and item features, allowing you to back up or move content between WordPress objections. Settings, of course, offer decisions to organize your site's title, motto, and time locale, as well as change examining, creating, discussion, and permalink settings. Tracking down an open door to research and modify these settings can deal with your site's show, security, and convenience.

Involving the Dashboard for Advancing Help

The WordPress dashboard furthermore gives decisions to perform standard upkeep tasks, like invigorating subjects, modules, and WordPress itself. Keeping everything invigorated ensures ideal security and execution. You'll get admonitions inside the dashboard when updates are free, allowing you to keep consistent over-site upkeep without any problem. The dashboard's concentrated control simplifies it to coordinate your site's overall prosperity, ensuring a smooth and secure client experience.

In overwhelming the WordPress dashboard, you open the most extreme limit of your site, enabling you to supervise content, plan, and settings easily. This focal sorting out clears a path for building a dynamic and attractive WordPress website that resolves the issues of your group and achieves your online goals.

1.3 Essential Settings and Configurations

Right when you've gotten to the WordPress dashboard, arranging significant settings guarantees your site works easily and proficiently. These settings cover all that from website page perceivable quality to interface structure, which impacts both client experience and webpage streamlining. Understanding and changing these secret plans will assist with fanning out a reliable early phase for future new development.

Coordinating Site Title and Brand name

Your page title and brand name are two of the fundamental parts guests see and anticipate a urgent part in depicting your site's personality. In the dashboard, explore to Settings > General to enter a title that mirrors your image or content and a brand name that sums up your site's motivation. A reasonable and convincing title and maxim likewise update your Web upgrade by motioning toward web records what's going on with your webpage. While these can be changed while, setting them early makes significant solid areas for an all along.

Setting Up Your Inclined in the direction of Time Region, Date, and Time Affiliation

Explicit time settings are fundamental for booking posts and time-interesting exercises, for instance, appropriating occasions or declarations. In the Settings > General segment, select your inclined in the direction of time area thinking about your locale or gathering. You can also pick how dates and times will be shown on your site, adding an impression of personalization. Setting the ideal open door district guarantees your booked posts convey at the best entryways, further creating liability and confining bedlam.

Arranging Permalinks for Web headway and Fathomability

Permalinks pick the improvement of URLs on your site. Overhauled permalinks add to client experience and further encourage Web progression by making URLs more coherent and watchword earnest. In the Settings > Permalinks area, select the "Post name" choice, which produces URLs thinking about the title of each post or page. This plan is cleaner and makes your affiliations bound to rank well in web search contraptions. Picking the right permalink structure near the start keeps away from likely issues with cut off joins on the open door that you switch arranges later.

Changing Examining and Show Settings

Examining settings control how your show page and presents are shown on guests. Go to Settings > Examining to pick whether your show page shows late posts or a static page. Picking a static page is a large part of the time strong for business or portfolio districts, while blog-organized protests could incline in the direction of showing advancing presents on keep content new. You can likewise control the amount of posts that are shown per page and set once-overs rather than full text for records, driving understandability and page load speed.

Arranging Conversation Settings for Client Obligation

The Conversation settings control how clients speak with your substance through remarks. Under Settings > Conversation, you can pick whether to empower remarks on posts, moderate remarks before they go live, and set up email rebukes for new remarks. Empowering remark offset stays mindful of worth relationship, as you can support or reject remarks thinking about importance. Changing these settings early makes a controlled, positive climate for swarm liability.

Regulating Media Settings for Ideal Picture Show

Media settings oversee how pictures and different media chronicles are shown on your site. In Settings > Media, you can portray default viewpoints for picture sizes, including thumbnail, medium, and colossal courses of action. By pre-arranging these perspectives, you guarantee consistency in media show, which upgrades the visual allure and client experience. Furthermore, further developing media points reduces record sizes, inciting quicker trouble times, which can sincerely influence Site smoothing out.

Setting Security and Web crawler Perceptible quality

To oversee web crawler noticeable quality, go to Settings > Analyzing and search for the choice to "Redirect web search gadgets from mentioning this webpage." Connecting with this setting is significant during the progress stage when you're truly making content and plan parts. Right when your site page is prepared for transport off, ensure this choice is uncontrolled so that web search contraptions can creep and record your page, making it discoverable by your vested party.

Empowering Secure Login with SSL

A SSL endorsing encodes information traded between your site and its clients, protecting touchy data. Many working with suppliers combine free SSL upholds, which can be locked in inside your working with dashboard. Straightforwardly following laying out SSL, declare that your WordPress settings mirror this by restoring the WordPress Address (URL) and Page Address (URL) under Settings > General regardless "https" rather than "http." This prosperity effort besides strongly influences your site page's Web improvement arranging, as web search devices base on secure regions.

Arranging Your Site's Email Address

Your site's email address, tracked down in Settings > General, is utilized for authoritative notice, for example, remark upholds, secret word resets, and updates. Setting an email you look at regularly is gigantic for keeping reliable site advancement and settling issues immediately. Utilizing an expert email address that matches your space likewise adds authenticity, especially expecting that guests use it to reach you.

Changing Your Client Profile

In the Clients > Profile locale, you can change your client profile, including your show name, bio, and profile picture. Setting up a total profile re-tries your joint efforts with guests as well as causes you to show up as a sound, open presence on your site. Your profile data could show up in changed puts on the site, including planner boxes on posts, adding a solitary touch to your substance.

Settling Fundamental Settings for a Smooth Beginning

With these fundamental settings arranged, your WordPress site is completely ready to convey a consistent encounter for both you and your gathering. From fanning out the site's visual person to additional creating comfort, these pivotal plans play a basic work in site execution and security. Fittingly setting up these parts will work with smooth future customization, improvement, and solid client obligation, setting you up for a useful WordPress experience.

1.4 Choosing and Installing a Theme

Picking and introducing the right point is colossal in fanning out the course of action and support of your WordPress site. A point facilitates the general look and feel of your site, impacts client experience, and effects site execution. In this part, we'll direct you through picking an ideal subject and the most notable way to deal with introducing it, assisting you with making an apparently enrapturing and utilitarian site concurred with your objectives.

Understanding the Significance of a Point

A WordPress subject closes the plan feel of your site as well as expects an essential part in comfort and client experience. The right subject upgrades your site's course, execution, and responsiveness, promising it looks skilled and works impeccably across gadgets. For instance, a clearly settled topic might be reasonable for a photography portfolio, while a moderate, text-centered subject could turn out to be better for a blog. Getting a subject that lines with your substance and gathering is fundamental for fanning out solid areas for a based presence.

Picking a Free or Premium Point

WordPress offers a huge library of both free and premium subjects. Free subjects can be introduced straightforwardly from the WordPress Point Rundown and give focal plan parts and handiness. Premium subjects, open from untouchable business places like ThemeForest or straightforwardly from point fashioners, occasionally go with extra parts, customization choices, and serious help. While free subjects are reasonable for fundamental districts, premium focuses could offer more significant flexibility and imperative game plan parts. Picking free and premium choices relies on your financial game plan, the complex idea of your site, and the degree of customization you require.

Seeing Significant Parts in a Subject

While picking a subject, search for significant parts that further foster supportiveness and solace. In any case, guarantee that the subject is responsive, meaning it changes perfectly across contraptions and screen sizes. Plus, subjects that deal Web engineering update improvement and speed streamlining add to higher web crawler rankings and better execution. A flexible arrangement is significant in the event that you need command over combinations, text styles, and association choices.

Expecting you mean to utilize online business esteem or incorporate electronic redirection, ensure that the subject sponsorships modules like WooCommerce and social sharing buttons. Perceiving these parts fairly early associates restricted down subjects that match your particular necessities.

Examining and Investigating Topics

You can examine subjects straightforwardly from your WordPress dashboard by going to Appearance > Topics and picking "Add New." Here, you can redirect focuses considering measures like standing, most recent transports, and highlighted subjects. Utilizing the "See" include awards you to perceive how each subject would look on your site, showing test pages, menus, and contraptions. Looking at sneak apexes outfits you with a thought of the subject's plan and worth, empowering you to picture how well it obliges your image and objectives. Many subjects offer demo content that you can import to test plans, providing you with a reasonable vibe of the point's genuine cutoff.

Introducing a Point from the WordPress Rundown

To introduce a subject from the WordPress Subject Rundown, go to Appearance > Subjects in your dashboard and select "Add New." Utilize the pursuit bar or channels to track down a point, then, click "Present" close to the topic you truly need to utilize. Once introduced, click "Approve" to apply the subject to your site. After incitation, the subject's course of action and improvement will uproot any past subject, permitting you to begin re-attempting the new arrangement. WordPress focuses from the record are generally particularly assessed for quality and security, pursuing them a solid decision for most districts.

Moving and Introducing an Unapproachable Point

In the event that you've bought a brilliant point from a distant source, download the subject report (overall a .pack record) from the seller's website page. In your WordPress dashboard, go to Appearance > Subjects and snap "Add New," then, select "Move Subject." Snap "Pick Record," select the point report from your PC, and snap "Present Now." When the establishment finishes, click "Lay out" to make the subject live. Two or three premium subjects go with extra modules or demo content, which could should be introduced unreservedly, constantly joined by unambiguous standards from the point supplier.

Tweaking Your Subject's Appearance and Plan

Just subsequent to endorsing your subject, you can change its appearance and design Evidently > Change. Here, you'll track down choices to change tones, printed styles, header styles, and that is just the beginning, reliant upon the subject's inherent highlights. Many subjects offer a live see, permitting you to see changes reliably prior to scattering them. In this part, you can besides add gadgets to sidebars and footers, set up menus, and make changes according to the site's general look. Re-attempting the subject guarantees your site mirrors your checking and rich inclinations, making an exceptional look that lines up with your objectives.

Actually examining Subject Responsiveness and Closeness

Prior to finishing your subject, test its responsiveness by overview your site on different gadgets, like work areas, tablets, and PDAs. Guaranteeing a smooth client experience across contraptions is essential, as adaptable use keeps on rising. Moreover, check closeness with key modules like Web creation redesign, security, and execution progress gadgets. Several focuses might be tricky with explicit modules or may require extra arrangement. Running these checks early partners you perceive and decide any likely issues, guaranteeing your site works dependably.

Remaining mindful of and Fortifying Your Subject

Exactly when your subject is introduced and transformed, it's principal to keep it resuscitated to guarantee resemblance with WordPress center updates and modules. Most subjects, particularly premium ones, discharge updates to additionally foster security, add new parts, and fix bugs. You'll get rebukes inside the dashboard when updates are free. Routinely empowering your subject frustrates closeness issues and keeps your site secure, guaranteeing a steady early phase for future development.

Through carefully picking, introducing, and yet again attempting a subject, you make a clearly spellbinding and important site that resounds with your gathering. Your point makes a way for client experience and plan consistency, assisting you with spreading out serious strong regions for a relationship while supporting your site's objectives.

Chapter 2: Designing for 2025: Themes, Layouts, and Aesthetics

Making a cutting edge, outwardly engaging web composition is more essential than any other time as web patterns develop. In 2025, web style center around spotless, practical plans that focus on client experience and commitment. In this section, we'll investigate fundamental plan components like subject determination, format systems, and arising configuration patterns to assist you with building an enamoring site that reverberates with the present clients.

The Development of Configuration Patterns in 2025

Configuration patterns in 2025 underscore effortlessness, openness, and responsiveness. Clients expect a consistent encounter across all gadgets, which has made responsive plan a standard component in many topics and formats. Perfect, moderate plans stay famous, with an accentuation on whitespace that further develops intelligibility and spotlights consideration on key substance regions. Moreover, variety patterns have moved towards hearty tones and muffled ranges that make a quieting, proficient tasteful. Movement plan components, for example, inconspicuous livelinesss and miniature communications, upgrade the client experience without overpowering clients.

Picking a Future-Evidence Topic

While choosing a subject, settle on one that lines up with 2025's plan standards and supports various designs. A future-verification subject is responsive, lightweight, and simple to modify. Subjects with worked in Website design enhancement improvement, openness highlights, and similarity with major modules will give a drawn out establishment to your webpage. Search for subjects that permit adaptability in plan, with various header, footer, and content design choices that you can adjust as your necessities develop. Numerous superior subjects offer high level customization choices, making it more straightforward to keep a cutting edge investigate time.

Embracing Framework Based Designs for Clean Construction

Framework based designs have become fundamental for putting together happy in an outwardly engaging manner. Frameworks give a reasonable construction, making it simpler for guests to explore and draw in with the substance. Numerous 2025 plans depend on multi-section frameworks that take into consideration adaptable arrangement of text, pictures, and recordings. This design additionally adjusts well to various screen sizes, improving versatile similarity. By utilizing frameworks, you make a firm visual pecking order that directs clients' consideration, making it simple for them to find what they're searching for without feeling overpowered.

Making a Consistent Client Involvement in Natural Route

Easy to understand route is a foundation of current web composition. As capacities to focus decline, clients anticipate that speedy access should data. In 2025, "tacky" route bars that stay apparent as clients scroll are famous on the grounds that they give consistent admittance to fundamental connections. Furthermore, dropdown menus and symbols assist with decreasing mess and further develop convenience. Focus on a smoothed out route structure with clear classes, so guests can track down important data in only a couple of snaps. Natural route increments commitment and decreases skip rates, emphatically influencing your site's exhibition and Website design enhancement.

Incorporating Visual Components with Effective Media

Excellent media, including pictures, recordings, and designs, add visual interest and improve commitment. In 2025, huge, high-goal pictures and full-width video foundations are normal in many topics, making a dynamic and vivid experience for guests. Visual narrating through media components can make your image message really convincing, particularly when matched with succinct, all around put message. Consider utilizing visual components to direct clients through the site, utilizing parallax impacts and unobtrusive movements to add profundity. Consolidating alt text for openness additionally guarantees that all clients, incorporating those with incapacities, can partake in your substance.

Involving Typography for Comprehensibility and Style

Typography assumes a key part in making a noteworthy brand picture and further developing clarity. Textual styles in 2025 incline towards sans-serif and moderate styles that are spotless and present day. Moreover, matching text styles with various loads or styles can assist with laying out a visual progressive system, causing to notice headings and other significant components. Text dimension additionally matters — bigger text dimensions are moving as they further develop comprehensibility, particularly on more modest screens. While picking text styles, think about the two feel and clarity, as a very much picked text style can improve the incredible skill and openness of your site.

Guaranteeing Openness for a More extensive Crowd

Site openness is fundamental in 2025 as comprehensive plan turns into a need. Planning for openness assists individuals with incapacities as well as works on generally ease of use. Many topics presently incorporate inherent availability elements like high-contrast modes, console route, and screen peruser similarity. Guarantee that every single intelligent component, similar to buttons and connections, are adequately enormous to be effectively clicked, and utilize graphic marks for better availability. By focusing on openness, you make your site more inviting to a different crowd, which can support traffic and commitment.

Upgrading Intuitiveness with Miniature Connections

Miniature connections are inconspicuous plan components that draw in clients by answering their activities, such as floating over a button or finishing up a structure. These little movements add a dash of intelligence without diminishing the principal content. Miniature cooperations are viable for directing clients, flagging that they've effectively finished an activity, or basically adding a lively component to the site. In 2025, miniature cooperations are refined to be unobtrusive and deliberate, making a drawing in client experience without diverting from the site's essential objectives.

Utilizing Dull Mode Choices

Dull mode is progressively well known in web composition because of its outwardly striking appearance and client interest for customization. Many subjects offer a flip choice for dim mode, permitting clients to switch in view of their inclinations. Dull mode decreases eye strain, particularly in low-light circumstances, causing it a positive element for guests who to spend extensive stretches perusing. It's an extraordinary method for adding an advanced, educated edge to your plan while giving clients command over their survey insight.

Settling Your Stylish Decisions for a Strong Brand Picture

Plan decisions in subjects, formats, and style characterize your image picture and impact client experience. By embracing perfect, responsive plans, open components, and the most recent design procedures, you make a cutting edge, connecting with site that hangs out in 2025's serious computerized scene. A predictable, outwardly engaging plan fabricates entrust with guests, keeps them drew in, and guarantees your site reflects current plan guidelines, laying out areas of strength for a for future development.

2.1 Modern Design Trends in 2025

In 2025, site synthesis plans will be client-driven and moderately feel considering support, availability, and striking encounters. From responsive associations to splendid utilization of combination and typography, plan plans underline straightforwardness and openness while conveying a charming client experience. This piece explores the most recent recurring pattern plan parts to move a drawing-in, future-organized site.

Minimalism with Purpose

The balance stays a striking model in 2025, with coordinators choosing clean associations, adequate whitespace, and smoothed out delighted to cultivate fathomability and concentration. The "calming down would be great" advance guarantees that objections stay simple to research, with just key data introduced in clear, consumable segments. A moderate plan improves stacking speed and guides the client's focus toward key substances, contemplating a cleaned wreck-free appearance. As opposed to stripping down all parts, 2025's control is associated with picking basic parts that raise the client experience.

Dark Mode as a Design Standard

Faint mode has moved from a client propensity setting to a game plan standard, offering an elective outline mode that decreases eye strain and searches remotely spellbinding, particularly on OLED screens. Different districts eventually come furnished with a crucial dull mode switch, permitting clients to flip between light and weak settings as shown by their propensity. Sketchers are cautiously considering arrangement contrasts in dull mode, making text and parts pop without picking clearness. Dull mode isn't just upscale but there of brain-to-client solace, particularly during the expanded investigation of social events.

Immersive Multimedia and Interactive Elements

The utilization of mixed media parts, including accounts, 3D plans, and normal parts, keeps on facilitating foster site liability in 2025. Full-screen video foundations, 3D activities, and VR-empowered highlights are turning out to be more open and prominent as web speeds move along. These parts make objections even greater and award brands to recount their story. Watchful parts, as limited scale advancements and float impacts, make little sense of liability, adding importance without overpowering clients. Downsized facilitated endeavors guide clients, straightforwardly showing practices like snaps or development segments.

Accessible, User-Centered Design

Straightforwardness has made it from a supportive part to a center fundamental for current districts. The plan that obliges to different client needs, like screen peruser closeness, console course, and high-contrast visuals, guarantees objections are broad for all guests, coordinating those with handicaps. In 2025, web pieces additionally coordinate parts like text angle flexibility and adaptable setups, engaging clients to tailor their audit information. This emphasis on inclusivity widens your gathering reach as well as constructs an addressing social responsibility.

Nostalgic Aesthetics with Modern Twists

Plan in 2025 sees recovery of a nostalgic feel, like retro massage styles, the smothered collection comes to, and uncommon energized symbolism got together with present-day plan procedures. This model joins the common characteristic of past styles with the comfort of the ongoing web rules, making an attracting exceptional discernment that resounds with swarms across ages. Coordinators join nostalgic parts to call feeling, while at the same time holding present-day structure and UX standards, accomplishing a reasonable and drawing-in look.

Advanced Typography and Playful Fonts

Typography impacts stepping and rationality, and 2025's game plans see a lengthy utilization of expressive, eye-getting text-based styles. Fashioners utilize outrageous, exuberant typography for titles and locales, appearing contrastingly as indicated by magnificent, simple to-look-at printed styles for body text. Variable printed styles, which change in size and weight competently based on screen size and client propensities, make typography more versatile. Text styles are fastidiously settled to remain mindful of lucidness across contraptions, giving a concordance between visual appeal and supportiveness.

Sustainable Design with Energy Efficiency

Adequacy in the plan has acquired significance as brands mean to confine their general carbon impression. Regions in 2025 spotlight on lightweight coding rehearses and further developed picture records to decrease energy use and further make stacking times. For example, upgraded plans with fewer assets and green working with choices assist with decreasing standard effect. A reasonable course of action interfaces with the client experience, where quick stacking and strong protests decline information use, helping both the client and the planet.

Emphasis on Personalization and User Control

Client personalization has taken a front seat in 2025, with objections offering choices to change plans, switch between dull and light modes, and change text viewpoints. Revamped encounters take novel thoughts of clients' inclinations and make an all the more uncommonly made experience. From adjusted thing thoughts to client express substance segments, districts are ceaselessly utilizing information-driven snippets of data to make charming, basic encounters. Permitting the client's command over interface settings further makes fulfillment as well as grows longer liability.

Data Visualization and Storytelling through Infographics

In 2025, information depiction stays outstanding as objections join frameworks, outlines, and infographics to pass on complex data rapidly and clearly. Infographics are utilized not exclusively to familiarize encounters yet besides with improve depicting, driving clients through a story that gets genuine factors along with apparently delighting parts. Persuading us regarding information acumen draws in brands to share snippets of data, making complex data more absorbable for gatherings and supporting liability.

AI-Powered Design and Automation

Man-made thinking (PC-based information) has changed into a significant piece of site configuration, connecting more adjusted and helpful encounters. Emulated information-driven plan gadgets help with making arrangements, further developing pictures, and tweaking content perpetually. Chatbots and electronic affiliations smooth out client support, offering help steady. Discerning game plan compelled by man-made information can in this way propose arrangement changes and updates considering client ways to deal with acting, keeping objections new and client-centered without requiring steady manual mediation.

Current game plan plans for 2025 are driven by an affirmation of solace, straightforwardness, and apparently staggering substance. By embracing these models, coordinators can make objections that resound with different gatherings, remain mindful of client obligations, and line up with current web principles. These game plan standards keep locales clearly dazzling as well as add to an anticipated and broad experience for all clients.

2.2 Selecting the Right Theme for Your Website's Goals

Picking the right subject is perhaps the essential push toward building a WordPress site that lines up with your objectives. Whether you're making an internet-based store, a blog, a portfolio, or a business page, the point spreads out the energy for plan and handiness. In 2025, there's a surge of exceptional subjects offering progressed customization, Web creation overhaul improvement, and minimized responsiveness. This part gives a manual for picking a point that best serves your site's objectives and further fosters the client experience.

Aligning Your Theme with Your Website's Purpose

Before jumping into subject choices, contemplate the essential occupation of your site. Expecting you want to fan out a blog, search for subjects with content-centered plans that pressure lucidity and stream. For an electronic business site page, based on subjects with coordinated shopping and things the pioneers highlight. Portfolio areas benefit from clearly astounding subjects with show and slideshow choices, while business objections conventionally need topics that give proficient plans committed districts for associations, client acknowledgments, and contact structures. By plainly portraying your site's objectives, you can channel topics that unequivocally address your necessities.

Prioritizing Customization and Flexibility

In 2025, customization is squeezing to make an excellent brand character. Search for subjects that permit wide customization without the essential for complex coding. Many subjects dealt with page makers, custom collection plans, and typography settings, which improve on it to change the course of action to match your image's look and feel. Adaptability in plan choices is similarly basic; pick a subject that gives different header, footer, and sidebar designs so you can collect so much that best serves your gathering. This versatility assists you with keeping one more look as your site makes.

Ensuring Mobile Responsiveness

With by far most of the web traffic coming from cell phones, adaptable responsiveness is non-asking to be disproved. A responsive subject consequently changes the arrangement to fit different screen sizes, giving a consistent encounter across work areas, tablets, and cells. Test a subject's responsiveness by exploring it on various contraptions or utilizing a topic demo. Responsiveness further makes client obligation, lessens skip rates, and genuinely influences Site improvement rankings, making it significant for giving a clear understanding to all clients, paying little heed to what their contraption is.

SEO Optimization and Performance

A subject's show can essentially influence your website page's Webpage upgrade and client experience. Lightweight subjects that heap rapidly will consistently rank better in web crawlers and give a smoother experience to clients. Search for subjects with worked in Web engineering overhaul streamlining parts, for example, clean coding, rapid stacking rates, and comparability with outstanding Web progression modules. Keep away from topics with extraordinary turns of events or irrelevant parts, as these can restrain your site. An especially streamlined topic manages your site's distinguishable quality as well as keeps guests related by reducing inconvenience times and managing overall support.

Built-In Features vs. Plugin Compatibility

While picking a point, evaluate its inalienable parts versus the comparability it offers with well-known modules. Several topics come stacked with highlights like sliders, grandstands, and custom post types, which can be useful yet may similarly affect stacking speed whenever misused. Considering everything, consider a lightweight subject with chief highlights serious strong regions for and with key modules like WooCommerce for online business, Elementor for plan, and Yoast Webpage smoothing out for improvement. Module likeness guarantees you the opportunity to foster accommodation without undermining your site's presentation.

Prioritizing Accessibility for Inclusive Design

Straightforwardness is consistently tremendous as additional clients depend upon regions that oblige different necessities. Select a subject that brightlights on straightforwardness, including highlights like control community course, screen peruser sponsorship, and high-contrast combination plans. Many subjects eventually coordinate choices to change message perspectives, alt-message for pictures, and ARIA (Open Rich Web Applications) names, improving on it to meet straightforwardness rules. Focusing on an open subject expands your gathering as well as shows your obligation to inclusivity, which can additionally foster your image notoriety.

Choosing a Future-Proof Theme

A point that is consistently empowered and kept up with by the organizer is the head for keeping a shielded, high-performing site. Search for subjects with strong regions for a record of updates, which shows that the organizer is based on remaining mindful of equivalence with WordPress center updates and security rules. Additionally, contemplate subjects from valid statement planners or business centers, as they as frequently as conceivable suggest help channels and documentation to assist you with inspecting issues. A future-check subject confines the bet of explicit issues down the line and guarantees your site maintains caution to date with the most recent highlights.

Considering Aesthetics That Complement Your Brand

Your subject's style ought to concur with your image character, making an intense look that resounds with your optimal vested party. Pick a subject with a variety of plans, typography, and plan choices that mirror your image's character, whether that is able, exuberant, moderate, serious solid areas, or. Revolve around subtleties like text style decisions and variety ranges, as they impact how clients see your image. A subject that supplements your image can refresh client trust, laying out a helping through association and further making liability.

Testing Themes with Demos and Reviews

Most top-notch subjects offer demos that allow you to investigate their elements and plans. Exploit these demos to concentrate on how the titles are up with your vision for the site. Investigate client audits and evaluations to get snippets of data into the subject's showcase, support quality, and any typical issues. The neighborhood can be basic in seeing focuses that have reliably performed well and helped others with accomplishing comparative targets. Testing and investigation assist with promising you to select a subject that will be solid and captivating to work with.

Picking the right subject is associated with evolving comfort, plan, and execution to make a site page that genuinely serves your website page's objectives. With careful thought of customization choices, responsiveness, Site improvement, and openness, you can pick a subject that meets both your energy needs and future goals, setting the establishment for a strong, drawing-in website page.

2.3 Creating an Impactful Layout

A strong arrangement is vital for organizing clients' thoughts, making an essential client experience, and supporting your site's motivation. In 2025, in-number arrangements are supposed to be clearly enamoring, simple to explore, and concur with present-day web rules. This part investigates the essentials of making an arrangement that resounds with your gathering, develops liability, and supports the objectives of your site.

Defining Your Website's Structure

An enormous association starts with an irrefutable, ordinary turn of events. Depict the crucial areas that your website page will coordinate, for example, the place of appearance, about page, associations or thing pages, blog, and contact page. Coordinate substance in a sensible stream that ganders at your chief vested party. For instance, a business site could focus on an association page, while a portfolio site would underline a show or part page. The improvement ought to allow fundamental to focal data and guide clients successfully through the site.

Emphasizing Visual Hierarchy

Visual solicitation is basic in assisting clients with understanding what's most enormous on each page. Use text perspectives, collections, and organizing to focus on key parts, like headings, joins, and convince (CTA) areas. More noteworthy headings draw thought first while isolating tones incorporate colossal joins or association focuses. Set up parts in a manner that consistently drives the eye, for example, putting the most fundamental substance at the top or in unmistakable bits. A solid visual organized development awards clients to see what's basic, further making course and developing liability rapidly.

Creating a Balanced Layout with Grids and Spacing

A reasonable arrangement depends upon trustworthy parceling, planning, and cross-segment structures. Different cutting-edge site association gadgets offer organization frameworks that assist with isolating the page into regions, which are changed and capable of guaranteeing parts. Sufficient dissipating between locales, pictures, and text further makes coherence and ruins the wreck. By sticking to a matrix structure, you can keep a trained professional and clean look that feels strong, whether in the work area or PDAs. Changed plans make your substance more absorbable, further creating client experience and keeping guests on your site longer.

Prioritizing Above-the-Fold Content

The "around the top" region, or the top part of your site discernible without examination, is where clients structure their initial feelings. This region ought to contain a convincing title, a short depiction of your site's motivation, and a reasonable CTA. For instance, a portfolio site could flaunt a legend undertaking toward the top, while an online business page could show something included or a plan proclamation. By focusing on strong substance around the top, you get clients an advantage and urge them to investigate further, spreading out the energy until the end of the site.

Implementing Effective Calls-to-Action (CTAs)

CTAs guide clients toward making unequivocal moves, for example, joining, buying, or reaching you. Position CTAs definitively all through the arrangement to draw in client-facilitated exertion without overpowering them. Use isolating varieties, serious text styles, or remarkable buttons to make CTAs stick out. Additionally, consider the communication of your CTAs — phrases like "Begin," "Sort out More," or "Get in touch with Us" convey clearness and centrality. Persuading CTAs assist with changing over guests into leads or clients, making them head for accomplishing your site's targets.

Optimizing Layout for Mobile Responsiveness

With adaptable traffic on the rise, making a design that performs well across gadgets is critical. A responsive arrangement changes with various screen sizes, guaranteeing messages, pictures, and gets are effectively open on telephones and tablets. Plan reduced plans with worked on the course, contact charming secures, and brief substance to cultivate solace also. Test your arrangement on different gadgets to guarantee parts show appropriately, changing depending upon the situation. A flexible streamlined plan further creates client experience, diminishes skip rates, and deals with the probability of guests returning.

Incorporating White Space for Clarity

A clear district, or void space around parts, is a solid area for an instrument that refreshes discernment and diminishes visual wreck. It withdraws content blocks, making it all the more clear for clients to zero in on individual areas without feeling overpowered. By unequivocally integrating void locale, you make an impeccable and formed plan that further makes the client stream and wisdom. Void locale in this way gives your site a front, complex appearance, assisting with underlining key parts and making a fair visual encounter.

Using Visual Cues to Guide Navigation

Clear signals, like bolts, pictures, or lines, subtly direct clients' ideas and guide them through the page. For instance, a bolt coordinating lower can enable clients to look, while a picture close to a CTA button causes them to see it. Breadcrumbs and pagination affiliations can moreover cultivate seminars on multi-page districts, giving way back to past areas. Noticeable signs update convenience by assisting clients with understanding where they are and where to go right away, working on the general stream and experience.

Testing and Refining the Layout

Exactly when you've fanned out your arrangement, test it to guarantee it performs well with your vested party. Direct client testing by get-together investigation from genuine clients to perceive how they assist with outing the plan. Appraisal instruments can assist with following how clients research the site, featuring regions where they contribute the most energy and any qualities of contact. Utilize this information to refine the arrangement, making acclimations to also encourage convenience, course, and obligation. Iterative testing guarantees that your course of action stays successful and lines up with your site's objectives.

Making an immense setup consolidates splendid status, from fanning out an unquestionable improvement to featuring a visual pecking order and planning a clear district. A particularly organized plan communicates with clients, further makes solace, and accomplishes your site's motivation, having a helping impression that urges guests to return.

2.4 Customizing Themes: Colors, Fonts, and Styles

Changing a point is a fundamental stage in making your WordPress site excellent and concurred with your image's personality. Developing tones, message unendingly styles could from an overall perspective at any point impact client experience, supporting your image's message and dealing with visual appeal. This piece investigates best practices for really tweaking these parts, guaranteeing your site stands isolated while keeping a firm and expert look.

Choosing a Color Scheme that Reflects Your Brand

The grouping plan is one of the main concerns guests notice, impacting their impression of your image. Start by picking central collections that address your image's character — whether that is strong and blazing or quiet and expert. Many subjects offer customization choices to change the shade of parts like foundations, buttons, headers, and affiliations. Pick a restricted extent of 2-4 tones to make congruity without overpowering clients. Consider utilizing corresponding or essentially indistinguishable from assortments, and confirmation there's sufficient division among message and foundation for significance. A certain combination plan fortifies memorability as well as makes an apparently satisfying encounter.

Using Color Psychology to Influence Users

Combination frontal cortex investigation can anticipate a legit yet strong aspect in organizing clients' feelings and activities on your site. For example, blue tones are routinely connected with trust and incredible ability, making them famous for business districts, while green conveys improvement and thriving, ideal for prosperity brands. Additional smoking combinations like red and orange can make a need to pick up the pace, making serious areas of strength for them CTAs. Utilizing combination with supposition further creates client obligation by making a character that lines up with your site's targets. Be mindful, regardless, not to misuse dynamic tones, as an over the top proportion of force can cause visual deficiency.

Selecting Fonts for Readability and Brand Identity

Printed styles are a fundamental piece of a site's style, adding to the two feel and discernment. While picking text styles, revolve around cleanliness — sans-serif text styles like Arial or Roboto are by and large more clear to analyze on screens, particularly for body text. For headings and subheadings, you should really consider a more undeniable scholarly style to add character, while keeping it connecting with the central body text based style. Take the necessary steps not to use more than two or three undeniable printed styles, as too many can make the site look jumbled and conflicting. Many subjects give worked in choices to change text styles, or you can utilize a module like Google Text styles for more prominent gathering.

Adjusting Font Sizes and Line Spacing

Text angle and line separating are desperate for clearness and straightforwardness. Titles and headings ought to be sufficiently gigantic to stick out, while body text ought to be smoothly huge without zeroing in on the eyes. Bet everything size of something like 16px for body text and keep a liberal line separating (around 1.5) to encourage lucidity moreover. Legitimate abstract style assessing and disconnecting assist with organizing clients through the substance, particularly on cells where more modest message can be attempting to investigate. Testing text perspectives across contraptions guarantees an open and easy to include understanding for all guests.

Customizing Styles for a Consistent Look

Consistency in styles, for example, button shapes, cutoff points, and picture channels, can lift your site's generally exquisite. Buttons, for instance, ought to have a uniform shape, size, and float impact across the site to make a firm plan. You could pick changed corners for a milder look or sharp edges for a more current, proficient feel. Moreover, apply a similar breaking point styles or picture channels for parts commonly through the site. By remaining mindful of obvious styling, you make a cleaned, bound together appearance that supports brand incredible skill and makes course customary.

Applying CSS for Advanced Customization

For those hoping to make further customizations past the subject's essential choices, CSS (Streaming Designs) licenses clear command over groupings, message perpetually styles. Utilizing custom CSS, you can change basically any visual part on your site, for example, changing the cushioning of parts, adjusting float impacts, or applying custom activitys. Various focuses give a custom CSS proofreader inside the subject choices, or you can utilize the WordPress Customizer. Information on CSS offers adaptability and awards you to refine your site's plan to extra immediately meet your snazzy and utilitarian targets.

Testing Color and Font Choices Across Devices

Collections and text styles can show up contrastingly across contraptions and screen sizes. It's fundamental for test your customizations on different gadgets, including work areas, tablets, and telephones, to guarantee a trustworthy encounter. For example, two or three tones could look more stunning on a telephone screen than on a work area, and certain printed styles may not convey precisely true to form on extra honest screens. Moreover, consider clients with collection vision needs by picking combination mixes serious strong regions for with. Testing and changing your game plan decisions for different contraptions further creates availability and guarantees your site looks skilled on all screens.

Leveraging Themes with Built-In Customization Tools

Different best in class subjects go with worked in customization devices, including combination pickers, text style selectors, and styling choices, improving on it to change your site without coding. These gadgets a significant part of the time merge live reviews, so you can see changes consistently going before appropriating. Utilizing subjects with overpowering customization choices smoothes out the game plan cycle and engages you to make serious areas of strength for a that lines up with your vision. This flexibility is particularly useful for clients without coding information, drawing in them to make monster plan changes easily.

Maintaining Visual Consistency Across Pages

A steady visual person across all pages fosters your image and gives a smooth encounter to clients. Apply similar varieties, printed unendingly styles commonly through your page, from the place of appearance to blog entries and thing pages. This incorporates saving an equivalent association for text-significant pages and reusing plan parts like fastens and pictures. Visual consistency upgrades client trust by making an expert look and assists guests with exploring the site naturally, truly as okay with the discernable signs and association plans.

Re-attempting combinations, scholarly unendingly styles assists you with making a WordPress site that feels excellent and changed. Through cautiously picking and testing these parts, you can plan solid areas for a clearly enrapturing site that reverberates with your gathering and really presents your image's message.

Chapter 3: Creating Content That Engages and Converts

Attracting and changing arranged content is vital for a site's success. In this part, we'll research the specialty of making content that gets visitors' thoughts along guides them toward taking needed actions, whether that is purchasing in, purchasing, or attracting with your picture. With a perception of your group, clear illuminating, and strong philosophies, you can make content that structures trust and drives critical results.

Understanding Your Audience's Needs and Preferences

Effective substance creation begins with a significant perception of your group. Understanding your goal fragment's tendencies, problem areas, and targets enables you to have content that affects them. Driving examinations, evaluating examinations, and attracting your group through web-based diversion can give critical encounters into their tendencies and challenges. Exactly when you tailor your substance to address express necessities, it ends up being more relevant and persuading, working on the likelihood of group responsibility and change.

Crafting Attention-Grabbing Headlines

The title is a large part of the time the essential part visitors see, and it is expected to be a critical part in choosing if they read. A strong title should be clear, minimized, and intriguing, enabling perusers to explore further. Use coarse speech, numbers, or requests to stir interest. For example, "10 Showed Approaches to Assisting Your Site's Change With Rating" or "How to Make Content That Drives Results" gets thought by promising huge pieces of information. Titles are an indispensable part of content philosophy, as they are set up for responsibility.

Structuring Content for Readability

The clear substance is basic to keeping visitors on the page. Sorting out happy with clear headings, subheadings, and short sections further creates intelligibility and makes it more direct for clients to check. List things, numbered records, and pictures separate huge pieces of text and element critical information. Using brief language and avoiding language similarly helps make the substance more open to a greater group. By organizing content really, you ensure visitors can quickly find what they're looking for, dealing with their experience and working on the likelihood of change.

Incorporating Persuasive Storytelling Techniques

Describing is a staggering resource for making an up close and personal relationship with your group. Sharing authentic models, client instances of defeating misfortune, or logical investigations can make your substance engaging and significant. Fruitful describing moreover incorporates presenting an issue, offering a response, and showing the constructive outcome of that game plan. Exactly when visitors can see themselves in the record, they will undoubtedly accept your message and feel convinced to take action. Stories refine your picture and give a setting to the value you offer, making your substance seriously alluring.

Using Visuals to Enhance Engagement

Visual substance, including pictures, accounts, and infographics, out and upholds responsibility by making information more absorbable and captivating. Huge pictures separate text and give a visual setting, while accounts give dynamic approaches to conveying ideas. Infographics can enhance complex data, making it more open and basic. While merging visuals, ensure they are brilliant, appropriate, and smoothed out for fast stacking. Attracting visuals gets through, further develops client experience, and further develops the likelihood that visitors will share or circle back to the substance.

Adding Clear and Compelling Calls-to-Action (CTAs)

Solicitations to make a move (CTAs) are central for coordinating clients toward changes. CTAs should be clear, action organized, and arranged definitively inside the substance. For instance, putting an "Upfront investment As of now" or "Figure out More" button close to the completion of a blog section gives perusers a speedy ensuing stage. Using tempting language that burdens benefits, such as "Get Your Free Helper" or "Start Your Outing Today," can make CTAs genuinely captivating. Attempting various things with different CTA plans, tones, and expressions can help you with sorting out what resonates best with your group and drives higher changes.

Optimizing Content for SEO to Increase Visibility

Rolling out satisfied that improvements over moreover incorporate making it obvious to web search instruments. Propelling your substance for Site enhancement by including significant expressions, meta portrayals, and alt text for pictures further fosters its situating on web search instrument results pages. Lead watchword investigation to recognize terms that your group is searching for, and unite these regularly into your substance. Web composition upgrade smoothing out extends your substance's detectable quality along with getting more assigned traffic, working on the likelihood of responsibility and change.

Engaging Your Audience with Interactive Content

Natural substance, for instance, tests, overviews, or number crunchers, offers a wonderful strategy for attracting visitors and keeping them on your site longer. This kind of blissful invites clients to share really, making a more redone understanding. For example, a test named "What Kind of Exhibiting Framework Suits Your Business?" can help clients find significant game plans while developing a sense of affiliation. Natural substance gets thought, empowers sharing, and much of the time prompts better change rates since it incorporates visitors directly in the experience.

Analyzing Performance and Refining Content Strategy

Effective substance creation is a nonstop cycle that incorporates looking at execution estimations and changing frameworks likewise. Use gadgets like Google Examination to follow estimations, for instance, online visits, skip rates, and change rates. Recognizing which sorts of content perform best allows you to refine your methodology and focus on what resonates most with your group. Testing different associations, tones, and topics can uncover significant encounters for upgrading content and achieving further developed results after some time.

Building Trust Through Consistency and Value

Consistency in quality and repeat of content structures depend on your group, arranging your site as a strong wellspring of information. Reliably dispersing significant substance, whether through blog sections, leaflets, or accounts, keeps your group associated with and upholds repeat visits. Giving significant encounters, answering ordinary requests, and keeping an eye on the most recent things shows that you handle your group's necessities. Exactly when clients trust your picture, they will undoubtedly change over, whether by chasing after your notice, making a purchase, or contacting you for organizations.

Making content that attracts and changes incorporates a blend of getting a handle on your group, presenting information effectively, and coordinating visitors toward movement. By executing these frameworks, you can encourage substance that attracts visitors as well as moves them to attract to your picture on an additional significant level, finally driving changes and building a devoted group.

3.1 Understanding Pages vs. Posts

In WordPress, content is coordinated into two organizations: pages and posts. While both can hold text, pictures, and media, each fills an alternate need and is organized contrastingly inside your site. Understanding the differentiations among pages and posts assists you with making a site that is both coordinated and easy to use. Here, we'll investigate the distinctions, use cases, and advantages of each to direct you in picking the right arrangement for your substance.

The Purpose and Nature of Pages

Pages in WordPress are expected for static substance, meaning they hold data that remains moderately unaltered over the long run. Normal models incorporate the landing page, About Us, Contact, and Administrations pages. These pages act as the foundation of your site, giving fundamental data about your image, mission, and contributions. Since they're not time-delicate, they commonly don't have distribution dates, and they are excluded from your blog's sequential feed. Pages assist with making a steady construction on your site, directing guests to the key regions that characterize your business.

The Role of Posts as Dynamic Content

Posts, conversely, are utilized for a dynamic substance that is refreshed regularly, for example, blog passages, news stories, and declarations. Posts are recorded backward sequential requests on your site's blog feed, with the most up-to-date happy showing up at the top. They're great for time-delicate data and content that forms after some time, similar to updates, experiences, or thought initiatives. Each post incorporates a distribution date and frequently a creator byline, assisting clients with following the most recent improvements in your subject matter. Posts likewise consider simple order and labeling, simplifying it for guests to track down related content inside unambiguous themes.

How Pages and Posts Impact SEO

Pages and posts can both improve your site's Website optimization when streamlined, however, they do so in various ways. Pages frequently rank well for designated catchphrases connected with your business or administration (like "Contact" or "About" pages), as they contain fundamental data that stays consistent. This static nature is useful for on-page Website optimization since these pages will more often than not gather authority over the long haul without requiring regular updates.

Posts, nonetheless, are powerful for focusing on additional particular, convenient catchphrases, particularly assuming you're delivering content around moving themes or industry news. The unique idea of presents permits you to catch search traffic from clients looking for flow data. Furthermore, because posts are essential for a blog feed, they frequently draw in more backlinks and social offers, which can contribute decidedly to your site's Website design enhancement.

Structuring Your Site with Pages and Posts

An efficient site uses the two pages and presents an easy-to-use insight. Pages act as your site's anchor, giving stable passageways to fundamental data. They are in many cases remembered for the fundamental route menu for simple access. Posts, then again, add profundity to your site by offering new satisfaction, making guests draw in and want more updates. Organizing your site with a blend of static pages and dynamic posts helps meet the different necessities of your crowd and gives them various ways of collaborating with your substance.

Categories and Tags: Posts Only

One of the remarkable highlights of presents is the capacity to sort and label them. Classifications bunch related posts into more extensive themes, while labels offer more unambiguous marks inside those points. For instance, if you run a way of life blog, you could sort posts into "Wellbeing," "Money," and "Travel," while labels could incorporate "Planning," "Health," or "Excursion Tips." These elements assist clients with finding related posts and further developing webpage routes. Pages don't uphold classifications and labels, as they are not pieces of the blog feed and are planned to remain solitary.

Customizing Pages and Posts for Branding

Even though WordPress subjects generally give a default design to pages and posts, you can modify each organization to suit your marking needs. Pages, particularly, take into account exceptional plans, as they frequently act as section focuses for your site and have to reliably mirror your image character. You could add custom headers, use mixed media foundations, or plan design varieties for various pages. Posts, in the interim, can be modified through individual highlighted pictures, post designs (like norm, display, or video), and format styles to make your blog feed outwardly engaging and locking in.

Comments: Engaging Through Posts

Posts ordinarily accompany a possibility for perusers to leave remarks, encouraging collaboration and local area commitment. This element is particularly helpful if you're running a blog where client criticism, conversations, or social verification enhances your substance. Pages, notwithstanding, by and large, do exclude remarks, as they're intended for more formal, static data that doesn't need client connection. By empowering remarks on posts, you welcome perusers to draw in with your substance and one another, which can further develop client maintenance and give significant experiences into their inclinations and considerations.

Deciding When to Use Pages vs. Posts

While choosing whether to make a page or a post, think about the substance's motivation and life span. For ageless, center data about your business, use pages. This incorporates static substance that gives fundamental subtleties or supports your image character. If you're sharing thoughts, experiences, or updates intended to be revived occasionally, a post is the better decision. This approach keeps your blog feed dynamic and permits perusers to get to a storehouse of data on different subjects.

Updating and Managing Pages and Posts

The two pages and posts can be refreshed, however the recurrence and way to deal with refreshes regularly vary. Pages require periodic updates as important to keep key data current, for example, refreshing contact subtleties or adding new administrations. Posts, in any case, might be refreshed or republished all the more as often as possible, particularly if you need to revive more seasoned content or keep it applicable with new information. WordPress offers simple administration for both, permitting you to modify content depending on the situation to keep up with precision and pertinence.

Understanding the extraordinary jobs and advantages of pages and presents engages you in sorting out your site. With the right equilibrium, you can make a WordPress site that is not difficult to explore, is profoundly useful, and draws in your crowd.

3.2 Building High-Impact Landing Pages

Welcoming pages are major for changing over visitors into leads, endorsers, or clients. Not in any way shape or form like standard pages or blog portions, a show page is reliably coordinated considering a singular goal, whether that is getting email addresses, driving a thing, or enabling workers for a web-based course. By focusing in on clearness, strong course of action, and key substance, you can cause welcoming pages that to further develop changes and help with achieving your business targets.

Defining the Purpose of Your Landing Page

A helpful show page begins with an evident explanation. Going prior to diving into arrangement, pick the specific target for the page. This reason could go from get-together email volunteers to prompting a bound time deal or showing something different. With an undeniable objective, you can tailor the page's plan, content, and wellspring of motivation (CTA) to work with visitors toward a specific outcome. Clear targets ensure that all bits of the welcome page participate unequivocally to make the potential aftereffects of progress.

Crafting Compelling Headlines and Subheadings

The title of a show page is usually the key part visitors see, and it needs to get their idea quickly. A persuading title should be restricted, attracting, and agreed with the visitor's assumption. Supporting subheadings offer a possible opportunity to add more detail or understand the drive without overwhelming visitors. For example, expecting that you're driving a free electronic book, your title could review, "Open Expert Tips on Appearing" with a subheading that says, "Download our free accomplice and gain methods from industry pioneers." Useful titles and subheadings give the page's central worth quickly, supporting visitors to research further.

Structuring the Layout for Maximum Impact

A welcome page's course of action should be great and obviously captivating, arranging visitors regularly toward the CTA. A valuable game plan by and large sorts out a cleverness stream: a title and subheading at the fundamental, a section highlighting key benefits, followed by affirmations, and a conspicuous CTA. Visual moderate design is fundamental for lead visitors' eyes beginning with one locale then onto the going with, chipping away at the page to check out and grasp. Using whitespace actually additionally ruins wreck, allowing each part to stand out and making the CTA the spot of mix.

Creating a Strong and Action-Oriented CTA

The wellspring of motivation is one of the most urgent bits of any invite page, as it's the entryway to achieving your change objective. The CTA should be recognizably shown and action coordinated, using phrases like "Download Now," "Get everything going Today," or "Seek after Free." The language should give a need to quit slacking or regard, inducing visitors to take a catalyst action. The button should stand separated clearly, using confining assortments and sufficient whitespace to promise it stands out. Placing CTAs in different regions on longer indications of appearance can likewise be convincing, as it ensures transparency without upsetting the page stream.

Highlighting Key Benefits and Value Propositions

Visitors need a specific impression of what they'll get by taking the best action on a welcome page. Use brief and benefit facilitated language to convey the urgent advantages of your idea. Rather than focusing in solely on features, highlight how the visitor will benefit. For instance, as opposed to saying, "Our thing organizes advanced assessment instruments," you could say, "Gain encounters that drive improvement with our solid appraisal." Outline things, short portrayals, and visuals help with conveying benefits quickly and truly, making the idea more intriguing to likely leads.

Incorporating Social Proof and Testimonials

Social authentication, similar to affirmations, survey, or trust undeniable pieces of proof, adds credibility to your show page by showing that others have benefitted from your arrangement. Counting an affirmation or two from satisfied clients can maintain visitors that they're going with an insightful choice. Video grants, client studies, or clear logos from clients add realness and spread out trust. By seeing that others have had phenomenal experiences, visitors will for certain confide in the value of your proposition and have a specific perspective toward creating over.

Using Visuals to Support the Message

Visuals expect a huge part in making a welcome page truly captivating and essential. Pictures, pictures, and records can cultivate the message and pass on the benefits of your thought quickly. For example, if you're pushing an electronic course, a short outline video can give encounters into the course fulfilled and quality, making it truly enthralling. Thing pictures, mockups, or legend pictures can in this way provide visitors with a much more clear energy of what they'll get. While picking visuals, ensure they're fitting, awesome, and agreed with your picture to show up.

Optimizing for Mobile Responsiveness

A high-impact welcoming page ought to be invigorated for all contraptions, as various clients will get to it on limited. Versatile responsiveness ensures that the page looks and works flawlessly across phones, tablets, and workspaces. Redesigned plans, contact fulfilling buttons, and clear printed styles update the client experience on extra veritable screens. While building or tweaking a show page, concentrate on it on various contraptions to ensure that all parts are shown unequivocally and that the CTA is easy to find and team up with on versatile.

Implementing Analytics for Tracking Performance

Right when your place of appearance is live, following its show is colossal for measure sound judgment and see regions for progress. Contraptions like Google Examination, heatmaps, or change following enable you to screen appraisals, for instance, weave rate, time on page, and change rate. Reviewing these evaluations gives encounters into how visitors are conversing with the page and parts any truly checks out at in the change way. By reliably destroying execution data, you can make data driven changes as indicated by extra develop the show page's impact and increment changes after some time.

Testing and Refining Through A/B Testing

A/B testing, or split testing, is a basic methodology for smoothing out show pages by isolating something like two assortments with see which performs best. Testing different titles, CTA tones, pictures, or plans can uncover what resounds most with your social event. For example, if one title makes a more significant number of changes than another, you can execute it to achieve furthermore made results. A/B testing is an anticipated cycle that considers reliable refinement, helping you with making a show page that is both generally useful and agreed with visitor tendencies.

An especially coordinated hello page, custom fitted with a sensible goal, strong visuals, and a strong CTA, can essentially help changes. By focusing in on client experience, social affirmation, and further made plan, you'll make points of appearance that drive results and effectively support your site's improvement structure.

3.3 Tips for Writing SEO-Optimized Blog Posts

Making web list organized blog entries is key for extra cultivating your site page's web crawler rankings and driving customary traffic. Web engineering redesign, or site improvement, consolidates causing content in propensities that to work on it for web search gadgets like Google to find, handle, and focus on your substance. With the right strategy for overseeing watchword choice, plan, and content quality, you can make blog areas that draw in perusers as well as rank well being referred to things. Here, we'll cover immense approaches to making web crawler organized blog sections that draw in perusers and help with accomplishing your page's discernible quality objectives.

Understanding Keyword Research

Articulation research is the supporting of web crawler arranged content. Watchwords are the pursuit terms your vested party uses to track down data, and perceiving these terms assists you with changing your substance to their necessities. Start by picking a major watchword that mirrors the main subject of your post and is pertinent to your gathering. Instruments like Google Watchword Facilitator, Ahrefs, or SEMrush can assist you with tracking down articulations with a decent equilibrium of search volume and contest. Right when you have your central articulation, consider related optional watchwords to integrate commonly all through the post, extending the post's compass while supporting the fundamental subject.

Crafting an Engaging and Keyword-Rich Title

The title is one of the fundamental parts web records and clients see, making it basic for Web progression. A particularly made title ought to combine your major watchword, obviously convey the subject of your post, and be satisfactorily convincing to draw in clicks. Plan to keep the title between 50-60 characters, as web crawlers routinely show basically the fundamental 60 characters in list things. Counting numbers, activity words, or an obligation of unequivocal advantages in the title (e.g., "10 Hints for Sound Living") can similarly make it more fascinating to perusers, dealing with the probability of snaps and obligation.

Writing a Strong, SEO-Friendly Introduction

A solid show spreads out the energy for the post and keeps perusers related with, yet it comparatively expects a part in Web smoothing out. Unite your central articulation inside the hidden 100-150 explanations of the show, promising it streams commonly with the substance. This signs to web records what's going on with the post and assists them with picking significance. Past watchwords, desire to shape a show that gets thought — mull over beginning with a solicitation, intriguing truth, or brief story. An impeccably made show helps Site with arranging redesign as well as broadens the potential results that perusers will remain on the page longer, a variable that strongly impacts search rankings.

Structuring Content with Headings

Headings (H1, H2, H3, and so forth) make your blog section more clear to investigate and assist with looking through motors handle the substance structure. Each post ought to have as of late a lone H1 tag, which is consistently the title, while subheadings (H2 and H3) separate the substance into segments, making it fathomable and worked with. Remembering your principal and optional watchwords for a few subheadings, where critical, can support the Site progression worth of these sections. Similarly, for the most part around facilitated headings further encourage client experience, working on it for perusers to find the data they're searching for, which can reduce skip rates and add to even more speedily look through execution.

Writing High-Quality and Relevant Content

Content quality is maybe of the most fundamental part in Web progression. Web crawlers base on satisfied that is informational, exact, and applicable to clients. Create by and large around satisfied that answers questions, gives experiences, and offers gigantic signs. Keep away from watchword stuffing, which can hurt Site improvement — rotate rather around utilizing articulations regularly and making content that offers genuine benefit to perusers. Longer posts (around 1,000-2,000 words) will routinely perform better in search rankings, yet guarantee that each sentence adds respect. Content that resounds with perusers will without a doubt be shared, related with, and returned to, all of which contribute strongly to Web sythesis improvement.

Optimizing for Readability

Clarity is a crucial piece of Web structure overhaul, as web search instruments consider client experience assessments while arranging substance. Write in a conversational tone, utilize short sentences, and keep away from language to keep perusers got. Detaching gigantic fragments, utilizing list things, and adding visuals where genuine all further encourage intelligence. Bet everything score that is reasonable for a general gathering, for example, a grade level of 8-10. Content that is not difficult to examine increments time spent on the page, which signs to web crawlers that the substance is critical and immense, maybe helping rankings.

Incorporating Internal and External Links

Counting inside and outside relationship inside your blog entries helps foster With glancing through engine improvement authority. Inside joins interface the post to other huge pages on your site, assisting clients and web records with exploring related content and working on the general improvement of your website. Outside connects with veritable sources add believability to your post and sponsorship any cases or information you notice, refreshing the post's faithful quality. Guarantee all affiliations open in new tabs to hold guests on your site. The two sorts of affiliations add to Web upgrade by making a catch of association that web crawlers use to record and rank substance.

Using High-Quality Images with Alt Text

Pictures make blog areas clearly astonishing, however they besides impact Website smoothing out. Counting critical pictures, (for example, photographs, infographics, or screen gets) further fosters the client experience and can chip away at the probability of offers through electronic entertainment. Each picture ought to have an overhauled record name and alt text — a short depiction that merges pertinent watchwords — to assist with looking through motors handle the picture's substance. Alt text comparatively further makes openness for clearly incapacitated clients, making a greater encounter and further supporting the post's generally Web improvement quality.

Concluding with a Strong CTA

Finishing your blog section with areas of strength for an of inspiration (CTA) is essential for client obligation and changes. A CTA urges perusers to make the going with step, whether that is seeking after a handout, inspecting related articles, or making a buy. Web search mechanical assemblies register client lead assessments, so entrancing CTAs that increment relationship with your website page can by implication furthermore encourage Web improvement. Make the CTA fitting to the post content and affirmation it's obvious without upsetting the stream. A solid CTA keeps perusers on your site longer, which can unequivocally impact web crawler rankings.

Regularly Updating Content

Content oddity is an arranging variable in Site improvement, particularly for subjects that change after some time. Dependably returning to and restoring more pre-arranged blog sections to add new data, update interfaces, or invigorate visuals stays mindful of importance and signs to web records that your substance is cadenced development. Restored posts routinely rank better and draw in recharged interest from clients. This approach guarantees that your blog stays a colossal asset, expanding its power and keeping perusers returning to your site page.

3.4 Multimedia Content: Images, Videos, and Interactive Elements

Mixed media content plays a squeezing part in making communicating with, dynamic blog segments that entrance perusers. Consolidating pictures, records, and savvy parts might from an overall perspective at any point further encourage client experience, decline skip rates, and update Site plan improvement by developing the time perusers spend on your page. Every sort of media fills a charming need, assisting with showing thoughts, separating text, and overhauling the substance. As you plan your blog sections, it's vital to see the value in the embraced techniques for utilizing mixed media genuinely to guarantee it supplements the substance and adds to the general peruser experience.

Adding High-Quality Images

Pictures make blog segments significantly more charming and can hugely redesign the client experience. Whether utilizing photographs, portrayals, outlines, or infographics, pictures give visual breaks and help with getting a handle on confounding considerations. To guarantee your photographs contribute firmly to Site improvement, utilize critical standard records that are compacted to remain mindful of quick weight times, as apathetic stacking can prevent guests and unfairly influence rankings. Likewise, each picture ought to have an enlightening record name and alt text. Alt text fills two necessities: it helps web records with understanding the picture content, further making Web smoothing out, and it additionally makes content open to obviously crippled perusers. Cementing enormous articulations commonly in alt text can in addition help your post's perceivable quality.

Embedding Videos for Deeper Engagement

Accounts are conceivably the best medium parts for holding swarm thought and adding importance to content. They are ideally suited for showing complex cycles, enlightening exercises, meets and portraying. Presenting records could increment anytime time spent on a page, which is a positive Site smoothing out signal displaying that clients view as the substance basic. While adding records to your post, guarantee they are great and material to the subject, and use attractive titles and subtitles. Working with accounts on stages like YouTube or Vimeo and implanting them in your posts can also encourage trouble times and make the substance more open across various gadgets. Counting a record or structure of the video's substance assists web search instruments with mentioning the video and awards perusers to skim for central issues.

Utilizing Interactive Elements for Enhanced User Engagement

Insightful parts like tests, reviews, sliders, and keen infographics can make a critical and interactive client experience. These parts enable peruser correspondence, causing the post to feel more re-tried and assisting clients withholding data. Regular substance likewise has critical strong regions for a part, as perusers will undoubtedly share, as a rule, drawing in encounters through virtual redirection. While adding keen parts, review openness and helpful equivalence; guarantee they work dependably on all contraptions and redesign the substance. For instance, a test that assists perusers with concentrating on their comprehension in regards to a matter can deal with their discernment and make an all the more clear insight. Adding regular parts absolutely inside the post can request that clients stay longer, exhibiting to web crawlers that the substance is huge and getting.

Optimizing Multimedia for Faster Load Times

While sight and sound can additionally foster client experience, it's indispensable for updating pictures, accounts, and instinctual parts to forestall slow page load times. Huge, unoptimized records can incite high weave rates and unfairly influence Web piece redesign. Use devices to pack pictures without losing quality, and affirmation video chronicles are worked with on outer stages to decrease weight on your site. For intuitive parts, utilize lightweight modules or items and cut off how much media chronicles on each page. Keeping load times under three seconds can assist with holding guests and further encourage your pursuit rankings.

Improving Accessibility with Multimedia

Making sight and sound open is key for arriving at a more prominent gathering and further encouraging the general client experience. For pictures, use alt text that portrays the substance unequivocally for ruined perusers. For accounts, furnishing etchings or records permits those with hearing inadequacies to make sense of the substance. Adroit parts ought to be very simple to explore, appropriate for screen perusers, and organized considering grouping differentiation and text angle for perusers with visual ineptitudes. By guaranteeing your mixed media parts are open, you make a more extensive encounter that can refresh client obligation and back Site smoothing out targets.

Enhancing SEO with Multimedia Captions and Descriptions

Adding inscriptions and portrayals to your media content is another persuasive Web upgrade practice. For pictures and records, more modest etchings can furthermore encourage mindfulness and add a setting. Counting watchwords customarily inside subtitles and depictions moreover assists web crawlers with understanding the media content, developing the potential results that your post will show up being referred to things for related questions. Similarly, inscriptions give perusers critical data that can additionally foster how they could interpret the post's central issues. Subtitles ought to be useful yet brief, assisting with figuring out without overpowering perusers with additional data.

Using Multimedia to Reinforce Your Brand Identity

Sight and sound substance are an incredible instruments for supporting brand character, as visuals can present tone and style. Constantly utilizing express arrangements, text styles, or stepped parts like logos inside your photographs, accounts, and shrewd substance creates insistence and supply with your gathering. Accounts, unequivocally, offer a technique for making an exceptional association, as may be obvious and heard obviously from brand delegates, making an impression of shared quality. By changing natural media happy with your image's voice and smooth, you work on the general cohesiveness of your site and sponsorship brand faithful quality.

Tracking Multimedia Engagement and Performance

Understanding how sight and sound substance adds to client obligation and Site improvement is fundamental for overhauling future posts. Use assessment devices to follow assessments, for example, time spent on a page, scroll importance, and video play rate. These snippets of data can assist you with checking which kinds of astute media resonate most with your gathering and make changes depending upon the situation. For instance, expecting you notice that posts with keen tests perform astoundingly well, you could need to set comparative parts in different posts. Seeing liability assessments likewise assists you with perceiving any potential stacking issues or comfort restrictions that could influence client experience.

Updating Multimedia Content Over Time

Equivalently as made content ought to be resuscitated consistently, sight and sound substance likewise helps by incidental sustains. Obsolete visuals, broken video joins, or non-working natural parts can diminish the possibility of your post and decrease liability. Dependably investigating your natural media content guarantees that all parts stay important, pivotal, and concur with the current course of action plans. By keeping media new and utilitarian, you keep a top-notch client experience and show web crawlers that your page is especially mindful of and dependable.

Chapter 4: Essential Plugins for a Powerful Website

Modules are fundamental mechanical gatherings that grow WordPress' center accommodation, drawing in you to change your site without requiring progressed coding information. With extraordinarily various modules open, picking the right ones is head for making a site that is significant solid areas for both competent. The Going with Locales presents the essential classes of modules and assesses how each can overhaul your webpage's showcase, security, client experience, and Site improvement.

Boosting Website Security

Security modules shield your site from normal dangers like malware, animal power assaults, and spam. Given the move in electronic dangers, it's key to put resources into a dependable security module to protect your information and your client's protection. Different modules give exhaustive affirmation, offering firewall limits, malware isolating, login assurance, and standard security studies. A couple of top modules in this portrayal combine Wordfence, Sucuri, and iThemes Security. Each offers consolidates that can assess for inadequacies, alert you to sketchy movement, and help with recuperating your site hoping to be it's compromised.

Optimizing for Search Engines

Web headway modules are huge for working on your page's recognizable quality on web search gadgets. These modules give devices to further develop page titles, meta portrayals, and watchwords, assisting you with arranging higher-in-list things. Yoast page improvement and In all cases, Web creation redesign Packs are well-known choices that guide clients in advancing on-page content, pictures, and clearness. They besides offer XML sitemap age and graph markup, which are sincere for web records to slither and deal with your page. Utilizing an Internet synthesis redesign module upgrades complex streamlining undertakings, making it all the more obvious to search for search rankings without anticipating that start should complete Web improvement information.

Enhancing Performance and Speed

Website page speed plays a pressing part in client experience and web page smoothing out. Execution streamlining modules, for example, holding modules, declines page load times and further encourages generally speaking site speed. Modules like WP Rocket, W3 Full-scale Store, and LiteSpeed Hold are eminent decisions that propose taking care of, record pressure, and drowsy stacking choices to redesign your site's show. Speedier districts will, when in doubt, have lower skip rates and higher change rates, so utilizing a presentation module is head for keeping guests pulled in and fulfilled. Furthermore, these modules permit you to change settings, drawing in you to find a concordance between speed and comfort or some likeness thereof.

Improving Image Optimization

Pictures are a significant piece of any site, yet gigantic, unoptimized pictures can restrain page stacking times. Picture streamlining modules like Smush, ShortPixel, and Imagify regularly pack and update pictures without surrendering quality, decreasing record sizes for speedier weight times. A couple of modules offer languid stacking, a technique that postponements stacking pictures until the client peers down to see them. This diminishes beginning weight times, further creating client experience and supporting Site smoothing out. By utilizing a picture improvement module, you can remain mindful of visual appeal while guaranteeing your site stays expedient and responsive.

Strengthening Backups and Recovery

Standard strongholds are fundamental for monitoring your site's substance. In case of information setback, a module that gives simple to-reestablish strongholds can keep you away from losing huge information or content. Support modules like UpdraftPlus, BackWPup, and Jetpack Backing award you to configure mechanized fortresses and store them on far-away servers or dispersed amassing associations like Google Drive, Dropbox, or Amazon S3. With a solid help module, you can recuperate rapidly from potential information difficulty accomplished by server crashes, hacking, or incidental destruction.

Adding Contact Forms for Better User Engagement

Contact structures are essential for drawing in clients to chat with you obviously from your site. Modules like WPForms, Contact Development 7, and Ninja Plans offer simple to utilize points of relationship to make special crafts, gather client requests, and gather data. A basic number of these modules similarly support mixes with email propelling associations, permitting you to make your endorser synopsis or gather information. A particularly organized contact structure module updates the client experience, as guests can contact you effectively without leaving your site.

Integrating Social Media Sharing

Virtual entertainment modules are valuable for adding social sharing buttons to your site, permitting guests to share your substance on stages like Facebook, Twitter, and LinkedIn. Modules like Social Snap, Shared Counts, and Brazen Social Arrangement give mobile social sharing buttons that line up with your image's game plan. These modules routinely combine assessment highlights, assisting you with following which posts are making the most obligation. By consolidating electronic redirection sharing choices, you expand your substance's reach and urge perusers to spread your message across their affiliations.

Simplifying E-commerce Functionality

For objections that coordinate electronic business restrictions, a module like WooCommerce is fundamental. WooCommerce is a serious solid area for a module that changes WordPress into a utilitarian electronic store, complete with stock association, segment dealing with, and flexible thing pages. With a tremendous library of expansions and combinations, WooCommerce empowers you to make a changed shopping experience that obliges your image. For complaints zeroed in on selling things or associations, an electronic business module smoothes out endeavors and guarantees a dependable shopping experience for clients.

Analyzing Website Traffic

Understanding your site's showcase is fundamental to improving and encouraging your site. Assessment modules like MonsterInsights, Google Evaluation Dashboard for WP, and Jetpack give snippets of data into guest direct, traffic sources, and eminent pages. These modules present evaluation information plainly on your WordPress dashboard, improving it to screen key execution markers without researching outside stages. By following and dissecting this information, you can go with informed choices on satisfied, plan, and publicizing systems.

Enhancing Content Management

Content association modules offer instruments for sorting out and showing content significantly more as a matter of fact. Modules like Elementor and Beaver Maker give chipped away at page-building accommodation, empowering you to make enrapturing associations without coding. For content-significant districts, TablePress and WP Table Architect can assist with showing information in worked with tables, while modules like Huge level Custom Fields permit you to make changed content fields. These modules give you more fundamental command over satisfied show, improving on it to oversee and show data that lines up with your objectives and further creates client experience.

Organizing these fundamental modules into your WordPress page guarantees that your webpage is streamlined for execution, security, Site improvement, and client obligation.

4.1 Top WordPress Modules for 2025

As we move into 2025, the WordPress natural system keeps on making, offering an expansive combination of modules that deal with your site's comfort, security, and execution. Whether you are building a blog, an electronic store, or a corporate site, the right strategy of modules can fundamentally moreover cultivate the client experience and smooth out association tries. Here is a gander at a piece of the top WordPress modules to consider in 2025.

Security Plugins: Protecting Your Website from Cyber Threats

Security stays a basic concern for any site proprietor, and in 2025, using strong modules that protect your site from consistently complex mechanized risks is tremendous. Wordfence Security keeps on being maybe of the most notable modules, giving solid areas for malware checking out, login security, and constant traffic checking. Another chief gadget is Sucuri Security, which offers site research, malware launch, and post-hack fixes. These modules guarantee that your site is secure, confining the bet of assaults, information breaks, and individual time.

SEO Plugins: Maximizing Visibility on Search Engines

In the cold-blooded scene of 2025, Web headway remains one of the most marvelous ways to deal with directing people to your site. Yoast Web improvement stays a go-to module for site proprietors hoping to redesign their web pages for web search gadgets. Its instinctual affiliation guide licenses you to change titles, and meta depictions, and make XML sitemaps while giving steady substance appraisal to furthermore encourage articulation use and fathomability. Another strong module is Rank Math, which is acquiring inescapability for its overall parts, like rich pieces, 404 seeing, and edge markup. These mechanical congregations are key for guaranteeing your site positions essentially being referred to things, expanding ordinary traffic, and discernible quality.

Performance Optimization Plugins: Ensuring Fast Load Times

Webpage speed is a major consideration in client experience and Site improvement rankings, and in 2025, further creating execution is a more serious need than any time in continuous memory. WP Rocket is a top-performing holding module that further makes site speed by empowering highlights like page taking care of, slow stacking of pictures, and instructive file improvement. For locales searching for a free other decision, W3 Complete Store is one more sublime choice that supports holding, minification of CSS and JavaScript records, and CDN mix. Utilizing these show movement modules can assist with keeping your site fast, decreasing influence rates and further making client fulfillment.

E-commerce Plugins: Streamlining Online Stores

As electronic business keeps on controlling the motorized scene, WooCommerce stays the top module for making a sensible electronic store. This module offers parts, for example, thing the board, segment entrances, stock following, and adaptable checkout processes. In 2025, WooCommerce augmentations permit you to orchestrate with unapproachable stages and foster your store's accommodation, for example, adding cooperation associations, selection areas, or obvious-level transportation choices. Other basic web business modules incorporate CartFlows for building high-changing over deals lines and Stripe for secure electronic piece managing.

Page Builder Plugins: Creating Custom Layouts Without Code

In 2025, making custom site arrangements without coding information has never been simpler, on account of serious solid areas for the majority of engineering modules. Elementor keeps on being maybe of the most well-known decisions, offering a dealt-with affiliation guide that licenses clients toward making refined pages without any problem. Its wide library of gadgets and plans makes it a versatile instrument for orchestrating inviting pages, blog entries, and, incredibly, whole regions. Another altogether respected page producer is Beaver Specialist, known for its direct spot of joint effort and capacity to rapidly make responsive plans. These page makers are head for site proprietors who need hard and fast innovative command over their site's plan without depending upon an originator.

Backup Plugins: Ensuring Data Safety

Standard strongholds are an irrefutable need to defend your site's information. UpdraftPlus stays a five-star support module in 2025, offering redid support booking, conveyed limit choices, and direct recuperation processes. It keeps up with various cloud associations like Google Drive, Dropbox, and Amazon S3, improving on it to store and recuperate your site's information. Another astonishing choice is BackupBuddy, which offers both manual and mechanized fortresses, and the capacity to impeccably move objections. With these modules, you can have assurance that your site will stay secure, regardless of whether there ought to be an event of information misfortune.

Social Media Plugins: Enhancing User Engagement

Virtual redirection coordination is vital for fostering your site's reach and drawing in with your gathering. Social Snap is one of the most amazing modules for 2025, offering flexible social sharing buttons, social follow attaches, and particular assessments on client obligation. Another outstanding choice is Ruler by Rich Subjects, which offers social sharing buttons, spring-up pleasing sharing plans, and electronic entertainment follow choices. These modules urge clients to share your substance on their electronic redirection profiles, assisting increase with making due, brand care, and overall obligation with your site.

Contact Form Plugins: Facilitating Communication

Solid correspondence with site guests is fundamental, and contact structures are one of the most excellent ways to deal with accomplishing this. WPForms is one of the top modules in 2025, known for using the enhanced interface and adaptable development decisions. It licenses you to make contact plans, studies, and email enlistment structures effectively, arranging dependably with email-propelling associations like Mailchimp. Another prestigious contact structure module is Ninja Plans, which offers progressed highlights like restrictive thinking, multi-step plans, and piece mixes. By adding a contact structure module, you can furthermore cultivate correspondence with your clients and produce tremendous leads.

Analytics Plugins: Tracking Website Performance

To gauge the consequence of your site and go with information-driven choices, assessment modules are head. MonsterInsights, a remarkable module for sorting out Google Evaluation with WordPress, gives beginning-to-end snippets of data into client direct, traffic sources, and prestigious substance. It additionally offers updated highlights like web business following, occasion following, and relentless information checking. Another module to consider is Jetpack, which gives both execution and assessment devices, offering a fundamental system for following guests, screening uptime, and dissecting liability assessments.

Image Optimization Plugins: Improving Site Speed and User Experience

In 2025, picture improvement is fundamental for extra making site speed and client experience. Smush stays one of the top picture streamlining modules, consequently compacting and resizing pictures to decrease report size without compromising quality. Other outstanding choices unite ShortPixel and Imagify, which likewise give picture pressure and lethargic stacking highlights. These modules guarantee that your photographs load rapidly and proficiently, assisting with additional creating generally speaking site page execution and Web engineering improvement.

Organizing these top WordPress modules into your site in 2025 will give you a liberal, secure, and particularly suitable page that settles the issues of the two clients and web search gadgets. Each module passes head parts on to redesign your page's show, client experience, and noticeable quality, guaranteeing your WordPress site stays serious in a persistently changing undeniable level scene.

4.2 Security, Speed, and SEO Optimization Plugins

In 2025, guaranteeing that your WordPress site is secure, fast, and advanced for web search mechanical assemblies is central for giving the best client experience, further making pursuit rankings, and watching your webpage from mechanized gambles. Involving the right modules in these key locales can have an immense effect on your site's show, security, and distinguishable quality. Coming up next are a piece of the significant modules to consider for redesigning security, speed, and Web creation improvement for your WordPress site.

Security Plugins: Safeguarding Your Website from Threats

With the rising rehash of cyberattacks, safeguarding your WordPress site is head. One of the most striking security modules in 2025 is Wordfence Security. This all-out module gives a decent firewall, malware isolating, tireless traffic checking, and login security. It helps block vindictive bots, defeats unapproved access, and gives no-fuss security reports. Another confusing module for getting your site is Sucuri Security, which offers site examining, malware launch, and post-hack fix associations. It correspondingly incorporates a web application firewall that safeguards your website from SQL blends, cross-website planning (XSS), and other destructive assaults. For added insurance, iThemes Security is another reliable choice. It offers highlights like two-factor affirmation, animal power insurance, and record change recognizing verification, which monitors your WordPress establishment for inadequacies.

By utilizing these security modules, you can guarantee that your site stays protected from cyberattacks, lessening the bet of information misfortune and remaining mindful of the trust of your guests.

Speed Optimization Plugins: Enhancing Website Performance

Page speed is essential in giving an anticipated client experience, further making web search gadget rankings, and diminishing weave rates. One of the top modules for making WordPress site execution is WP Rocket. This holding module is not difficult to utilize and offers several highlights, for example, page taking care of, picture drowsy stacking, instructive record redesign, and GZIP pressure. WP Rocket in addition keeps up with content development affiliations (CDN) to serve static files quicker, diminishing burden times essentially.

For those searching for a free other decision, the W3 scale Store is a significant solid area that supports holding, minification of CSS and JavaScript records, and coordinates with CDNs. It speeds up your site by reducing the server load and further making page load times. Autoptimize is another awe-inspiring module for moving your site's speed. It is based on working on the code by cementing, minifying, and saving items and configurations, further making execution. Smush is similarly a critical module for accelerating your site by compacting and resizing pictures without undermining their quality. Pictures routinely address a fundamental piece of a site's heap time, and Smush lessens their record size while remaining mindful of visual constancy.

Together, these speed overhaul modules assist with guaranteeing that your website page stacks rapidly, giving a preferable encounter over guests and further cultivating your site page's, when in doubt, smoothing out.

SEO Optimization Plugins: Improving Search Engine Rankings

Site improvement (Web smoothing out) is essential for stretching out ordinary traffic to your WordPress page. Yoast Web engineering redesign keeps on being one of the most striking and persuading modules for Website upgrade improvement in 2025. It assists you with moving your site's meta marks, including titles and portrayals, makes XML sitemaps, and guarantees your substance is justifiable and watchword streamlined. Yoast besides offers progressed highlights like breadcrumb course, plan markup, and online redirection coordination, which can additionally foster your Internet organization overhaul endeavors.

Another astounding Site improvement module is Rank Math, which has acquired obvious quality for grasping the mark of connection and components basic. Rank Number related gives on-page Web progression assessment, articulation following, and blends in with Google Search Control center. It also offers progressed highlights, for example, rich pieces, nearby Site smoothing out instruments, and a substance PC-based knowledge consolidation that works on satisfaction for better arranging. Regardless of your perspective Site smoothing out Pack is a solid area for another, particularly for amateurs. It works on Web piece updates by furnishing direct game-plan choices and getting along with online entertainment stages, XML sitemaps, and web page plan improvement for custom post types.

For specific Web progression, Plan Star is an uncommon module that adds diagram markup to your site, which assists web search instruments with figuring out your substance better. This can incite better perceptible quality by being referred to as things with rich pieces, which show extra data like appraisals, audits, and occasion subtleties straightforwardly in web search device postings.

Joining this Internet organization redesign streamlining modules with exceptional substance methodology will assist with managing your page's rankings, increment typical traffic, and give a preferred encounter over guests by guaranteeing that your substance is discoverable and particularly planned.

Combining Security, Speed, and SEO Plugins for a Powerful Website

Coordinating the right security, speed, and Web structure update improvement modules into your WordPress site page in 2025 can give serious solid areas for that upgrades client experience, protects your website page from dangers, and lifts your perceivable quality on web search gadgets. Security modules like Wordfence and Sucuri keep your site safeguarded, while speed movement modules like WP Rocket and Smush guarantee quick stacking times. Web improvement modules like Yoast Site improvement and Rank Numerical work on it to move your webpage for web records, driving more customary traffic.

By picking and arranging the right strategy of modules, you can make a page that isn't at this point essentially secure and quick what's more improved for web search gadget execution, offering your guests a consistent and interactive experience. With the reliably causing advanced situation, maintaining caution to date with the most recent module parts and best practices here will assist with keeping your site serious in 2025 no doubt.

4.3 E-commerce, Analytics, and Social Media Integration

In 2025, the capacity to work with online business highlights, track site execution, and effect virtual redirection arranges dependably into your WordPress website page is major for encouraging your electronic presence, developing changes, and refreshing client obligations. To fabricate a useful page, particularly in the event that you're keeping a business or an internet based store, squeezing to use modules work with smooth web business endeavors, give completely evaluation, and help with coordinating virtual redirection affiliations. Under, we research how to coordinate these parts into your WordPress site indeed.

E-commerce Integration: Building a Seamless Online Store

Arranging web business esteem into your WordPress page is fundamental to selling things or associations on the web. WooCommerce stays the important web-based business module for WordPress in 2025. This strong module licenses you to accumulate and deal with an online store without any problem. WooCommerce gives highlights like stock association, secure piece entryways, conveying choices, and client the board. With an expansive collection of additional things, you can expand the comfort of your online store, whether you're selling genuine articles, electronic downloads, or benefits.

For those searching for extra parts, Shopify Purchase Button is a remarkable other decision. It draws in you to coordinate your Shopify store with your WordPress site, permitting you to implant things or thing mixes straightforwardly onto your pages. For selling motorized things, Direct Undeniable level Downloads is an extraordinary choice, giving an essential technique for overseeing and sell advanced stock like programming, electronic books, or music.

While building an internet based business webpage page, it's fundamental to have a general client experience. Changing the store setup, thing pages, and checkout process is fundamental. Modules, for example, Elementor contemplate regular course of action, working on it to make an apparently enamoring electronic store. Moreover, arranging segment areas like Stripe or PayPal guarantees secure exchanges for your clients, dealing with their trust and supporting change rates.

Analytics Integration: Tracking Website Performance

Following site execution is fundamental for figuring out client lead, evaluating achievement, and settling on information driven choices to work on your site. Google Appraisal for WordPress by MonsterInsights is one of the most notable modules for putting together Google Assessment concerning your WordPress site. It awards you to accommodatingly follow site traffic, client obligation, electronic business execution, starting there, the sky is the limit. The module works on the most generally perceived way to deal with adding following code to your site, giving you snippets of data into where your guests are coming from, what pages they are drawing in with, and how they are connecting with your substance.

For additional point by point snippets of data, Matomo Assessment offers a choice to explore Evaluation. Matomo gives more command over your information and offers progressed highlights like heatmaps, meeting records, and change following. Another huge assessment module is Jetpack, which gives site nuances, accessible energy checking, and, amazingly, beast force affirmation, guaranteeing that you can follow execution while keeping your site secure.

Using these assessment mechanical congregations will permit you to arrive at informed outcome about managing your site, changing propelling structures, and updating client experience by understanding what works and what doesn't.

Social Media Integration: Connecting with Your Audience

Online entertainment mix is key for directing people to your site and drawing in with your gathering. Modules like Social Snap and Ruler assist with coordinating social sharing buttons into your site, permitting clients to share content on stages like Facebook, Twitter, LinkedIn, and Instagram. Social Snap additionally offers highlights like web based redirection follow buttons, social login choices, and assessment to follow how your substance is performing across various stages.

Furthermore, Instagram Feed awards you to show your Instagram posts straightforwardly on your site, giving areas of strength for a for including your electronic redirection content. Merging virtual entertainment feeds can request that guests follow your social records, developing liability and giving new bright on your site. Restore Old Posts is another significant module that in this manner shares your old substance to online entertainment, keeping your social profiles dynamic and driving traffic back to your page.

For overseeing electronic redirection missions, Cushion or Hootsuite mixes can be huge. These stages permit you to configuration posts, track liability, and screen execution across various web based entertainment channels from one dashboard. With these instruments, you can robotize your web-based redirection propelling endeavors, guaranteeing that your site unquestionably stands separated it merits while saving time for different undertakings.

Integrating All Three Components for Maximum Impact

Right when you join web business, evaluation, and online redirection solidifications, you are making a site page that drives deals as well as points of interaction with guests, gives critical snippets of data, and broadens your appear at across heartfelt stages. For example, following electronic business execution with Google Evaluation or Matomo assists you with perceiving which things are performing awesome, and which need improvement, drawing in you to overhaul your advancing systems.

By solidifying social sharing buttons and feeds, you can maintain client participation with your substance and store, driving more traffic and sensible clients to your site. Simultaneously, having on the web business esteem like WooCommerce or Essential Modernized Downloads guarantees a consistent web shopping experience that lines up with your propelling endeavors, giving an expansive client experience from exposure to buy.

In light of everything, sorting out internet based business, evaluation, and virtual redirection into your WordPress site page in 2025 assists you with making a truly stunning, quantifiable, and valuable electronic presence. By picking the right modules and contraptions for these key regions, you can update the general client experience, seek after information driven choices to further develop execution, and confirmation that your page is prepared for bring about the essentially serious internet based business local area.

4.4 How to Install, Configure, and Manage Plugins

Introducing, arranging, and controlling modules is a central dominance for any WordPress client, as modules add basic comfort to your site without requiring custom coding. In this part, we'll cover the critical stages to introduce modules from the WordPress vault, plan their settings, and successfully direct them to remain mindful of ideal site execution and security.

Installing Plugins: Methods and Best Practices

Introducing a module is prompt, and WordPress offers two or three strategies to do within that limit. The most eminent way is to utilize the WordPress Module Storage space. To introduce a module from this storeroom, explore your WordPress Dashboard, go to Plugins > Add New, and utilize the pursuit bar to find the module you want. Right when you find it, click Present Now, and after establishment, select Begin to empower the module.

Another methodology is to move a module really, which is particularly significant for premium modules that aren't open in the WordPress storage space. To move a module, go to Plugins > Add New and click on the Trade Module button at the most important characteristic of the page. From here, select the Pack record of the module from your PC, click Present Now, and once moved, begin it. This strategy ponders more essential adaptability in picking modules that course of action progressed or centered functionalities.

For extra-made clients, modules can in addition be introduced through FTP by moving the module records straightforwardly to the wp-content/modules organizer on your server. Once moved, go to the Modules page on your dashboard to enact the module. These systems offer adaptability thinking about your necessities and the wellsprings of your modules.

Configuring Plugins: Setting Up for Optimal Performance

After establishment, arranging your module settings is fundamental to guarantee that it capacities as per your particular necessities. Each module has unprecedented arrangement choices, which are typically tracked down in another menu thing inside your WordPress dashboard. For instance, assuming you've introduced a Web improvement module like Yoast, you'll see another Internet structure redesign menu where you can change settings related to Meta marks, XML sitemaps, and virtual redirection sharing.

While coordinating modules, it's basic to follow any arrangement wizards that the module gives, as these reliably guide you through the essential game plan steps. For instance, WP Rocket (a taking care of module) has an arrangement wizard that licenses you to rapidly empower saving and lethargic stacking. Utilizing these arrangement guides guarantees that you are including the proposed settings for execution and worth.

Furthermore, guarantee that you survey the module documentation. Different modules go with a coordinated help piece or online documentation that makes with distinguishing each setting. This is especially enormous for complex modules with various customization choices. Finding an astonishing entryway to get a handle on the settings allows you to change the module to meet your particular necessities, which can furthermore encourage both the client experience and site execution.

Managing Plugins: Updates, Deactivation, and Deletion

Guiding modules is major to keeping a quick, secure, and utilitarian site. Routinely fortifying modules is crucial, as updates constantly incorporate security patches, execution redesigns, and new parts. To stimulate a module, examine the Modules page on your dashboard, where you'll see a section for any modules with open updates. Click Update Now to introduce the most recent variety. On the other hand, you can connect with altered resuscitates by picking this choice under each module, which can be significant for guaranteeing fundamental modules maintain caution to date.

On the off chance that you want to deactivate a module, maybe for investigating or to moreover cultivate site execution, essentially go to the Modules page, find the module, and snap Deactivate. This activity holds the module back from running yet keeps it introduced, permitting you to reactivate it later if fundamental. Deactivating modules that you're not utilizing can assist with accelerating your site and decrease the bet of fights with various modules or subject restores.

To everlastingly clear out a module, go to the Modules page, deactivate it on the off chance that it's dynamic, and select Erase. This move initiates the module documents from your server, opening up space and maybe further making site execution. In any case, review that killing a module may also forgo its associated settings and information. For modules that store fundamental information, contemplate sponsorship up your site before annihilation.

Best Practices for Plugin Management: Avoiding Conflicts and Optimizing Performance

Utilizing such innumerable modules can incite debates and tone down your site. Along these lines, it's ideal to introduce essentially the modules that are vital for your site's worth. Accepting two modules fills comparable prerequisites, pick the one that best purposes your issues and uninstall the other to decrease the bet of fights. Moreover, stay away from old modules that haven't been fortified of late, as these can present security deficiencies.

Dependably researching your modules is a fair practice. At standard ranges, audit the modules you have introduced and pick if they are as of now critical. Tolerating you see that you are done utilizing explicit modules, deactivating and erasing them can assist with smoothing out your site.

At long last, consider utilizing a module execution screen like the Solicitation Screen. This gadget allows you to see which modules are consuming the most assets, assisting you with perceiving any show bottlenecks accomplished by unambiguous modules. By seeing module execution, you can guarantee that your site stays quick and fit.

Building a Powerful Website with Thoughtful Plugin Management

Introducing, sorting out, and managing modules genuinely permits you to bridle the whole of WordPress without compromising site execution or security. By following the suggested methods for the establishment, remaining steady with restores, and confining how many unique modules, you can keep a fast and secure WordPress site in 2025.

Chapter 5: Advanced Customization with Gutenberg and Page Builders

As of late, WordPress has framed to change into an essentially flexible stage for customization, because of the Gutenberg supervisor and prominent page creators. These instruments permit clients to make particularly different, fit-looking districts without wanting to shape code. In this part, we'll plunge into cutting-edge customization frameworks utilizing Gutenberg and outstanding page creators like Elementor, Divi, and Beaver Architect. Overpowering these contraptions, you can assemble complex designs, combine hand-made parts, and redesign the client experience.

Understanding Gutenberg: Beyond Basic Blocks

Gutenberg, the default WordPress block chief, was introduced in WordPress 5.0 as a component to manage satisfied creation through a particular framework. Gutenberg utilizes "blocks" to create and organize content, empowering you to add text, pictures, records, buttons, and custom contraptions. Notwithstanding, to open its most outrageous breaking point, you want to investigate progressed blocks and parts.

In 2025, Gutenberg has combined obvious level blocks and settings, for example, reusable blocks, custom block designs, and settled blocks, which make it conceivable to make complex page arrangements. Reusable blocks allow you to save a particular block plan or plan and use it across various pages. This part is particularly huge for site parts like a wellspring of inspiration areas or contact structures, where consistency across pages is essential. Custom block plans, in the meantime, empower you to make a library of design designs you can embed into any page, assisting with smoothing out the planning cycle.

Furthermore, unapproachable modules like Kadence Blocks or Stackable give more disease block choices, like huge level picture shows, surveying tables, and reinvigorated parts. These modules expand Gutenberg's capacities, making it conceivable to make captivating and sharp page plans with unimportant exertion.

Customizing with Page Builders: Key Features and Flexibility

While Gutenberg is strong, serious page engineers like Elementor, Divi, and Beaver Producer take customization significantly further by offering a more prominent degree of plan choices and an extraordinarily instinctual normal characteristic of participation. Page creators go with set-up plans, progressed styling choices, and the capacity to helpfully change settings for work areas, tablets, and minimal grandstands, which is sincere for the responsive course of action.

Elementor, for example, offers wide contraption choices, from direct text boxes to complex picture merry-go-rounds and honors. Besides united progressed with highlights like advancement impacts, custom orchestrating, and working in plan contraptions. With Elementor, you can indeed add parts like parallax exploring, enabled titles, and point foundations, refreshing the visual appeal of your site.

Divi, another outstanding page maker, offers a predictable, front-end changing experience, permitting you to see changes as you make them. Divi in this way combines strong plan choices, for example, custom CSS fields, split testing, and a titanic library of plan parts. This maker is especially valuable for those hoping to make a surprising site state-of-the-art, as it empowers essentially no-fuss customization at each level.

Choosing Between Gutenberg and Page Builders

The decision between Gutenberg and a page producer constantly relies on your undertaking needs, explicit limits, and money-related plans. Gutenberg is made into WordPress, lightweight, and plausible with an expansive variety of modules, making it ideal for clients who need a prompt, moderate arrangement. Likewise, since it's basic for the WordPress center, regions worked with Gutenberg will generally stack speedier than those energetically dependent upon distant page creators.

Regardless, if you're betting on everything or groundbreaking setups, a serious page fashioner may be more reasonable. Creators like Elementor and Divi offer more game plan flexibility and customization highlights than Gutenberg. Page engineers are comparatively especially valuable for clients who need coding limits at any rate need to make proficient, eye-getting regions.

Enhancing Functionality with Add-Ons and Integrations

To take advantage of Gutenberg or any page maker, investigate additional things and blends that broaden their worth. For instance, Ludicrous Addons for Elementor and PowerPack Addons for Elementor give a degree of extra contraptions, including commencement tickers, info boxes, and custom merry-go-rounds. Divi moreover hosts different third-gathering modules, including premium modules like Divi Otherworldly, which adds creative parts like popup modals, text activities, and flip boxes.

These additional things allow you to draw in objections that give guests a consistent, striking experience. Whether you're including a commencement clock for an approaching occasion or making cunning parts like tabs and accordions, additional things can essentially deal with your site's comfort and understanding without requiring broad coding information.

Optimizing Performance: Balancing Design and Speed

While page engineers offer dumbfounding customization limits, they can similarly add swell to your site in the event that not utilized cautiously. It's fundamental for redesign execution to guarantee your site stays quick and responsive. Try not to over-inconvenient your pages with such endless parts, as absurd substance can restrain page stacking times. Also, some page makers offer choices to stack critical CSS and JavaScript records, decreasing the heap on your site.

To keep a smooth client experience, you can comparably utilize modules like WP Rocket for taking care of and Autoptimize for compacting CSS and JavaScript reports. These contraptions work with page architects to furthermore make stacking times by minifying code, empowering lethargic stacking, and updating picture reports. Making these strides will assist you with finding a concordance between visual appeal and valuable site execution or the like.

Mastering Advanced Customization for a Unique Website

By furnishing the general furthest reaches of Gutenberg and page makers, you can plan a bleeding edge, and partner with a site that hangs out in 2025. Each contraption offers striking benefits: Gutenberg gives a lightweight, worked-with strategy, while page makers like Elementor and Divi offer a wide plan an open door, and worth. Whether you pick Gutenberg, a page engineer, or a blend of both, understanding their capacities awards you to make an expert site that lines up with your vision, keeps up with your objectives, and conveys an uncommon client experience.

5.1 Mastering the Gutenberg Editor

The Gutenberg boss is critical strong regions for a contraption framed clearly into WordPress, making it possible to make a rich substance with top-tier plan features — all without code. Since its show, Gutenberg has changed WordPress by allowing clients to create pages with blocks, making it a go-to instrument for content producers, bloggers, and page experts the equivalent. This part will guide you through Gutenberg's key components, clear-level customization decisions, and best practices for making invigorating, responsive substance.

Exploring the Core Features of Gutenberg Blocks

At the point of convergence of Gutenberg are blocks — disengaged parts can be added, changed, and yet again attempted to push toward any page plan. Each block fills a specific need, whether it's for text, pictures, gets, or sight and sound substance. The central directions community blocks stray pieces like segments, headings, pictures, and records, as well as extra normal parts, like introductions, sections, and gets. Gutenberg's block-based approach gives adaptability to making anything from clear blog segments to perplexing greetings pages.

Gutenberg's flexibility is also updated by its boss on handiness, which licenses you to modify blocks on the page, enabling consistent affiliation changes. For those familiar with visual editors, this part offers a trademark, plan warm experience that rates up fulfilled creation.

Using Reusable and Custom Block Patterns

Potentially the most shocking part of Gutenberg is the Reusable Blocks decision, which allows you to save any organized block as a design that can be reused across various pages or posts. For example, if you have a specific wellspring of motivation fragments or a styled affirmation block, saving it as a reusable block ensures clear styling across your site. This part is especially colossal for affiliations that stay aware of brand consistency or repeat similar substance parts across their pages.

Gutenberg likewise stays aware of custom block plans and sets up block designs that can be installed with a singular snap. WordPress consolidates a blend of block plans out of the compartment, yet you can equivalently make your own or present far-off models through modules. Custom block plans license you to set up complex affiliations, saving time while saving your site's strong regions for strategy on-brand quickly.

Advanced Block Settings for Greater Design Control

While the default blocks in Gutenberg are very simple to use, they in this way go with state-of-the-art customization decisions that provide you more tremendous control over their appearance and strength. Each block joins a settings board on the right-hand side, where you can change decisions like typography, gathering, and dispersing. For example, you can really impact message points of view, add custom edges, and apply establishment tones to message blocks.

A few blocks, like pieces and social gatherings, have extra unendingly plan settings, allowing you to make multi-part fragments that change well to various screen sizes. Besides, for pictures and records, you can attract unfeeling stacking to smooth out page speed, an urgent part of complaints that emphasize execution.

Enhancing Functionality with Third-Party Block Plugins

While Gutenberg's inherent blocks are flexible, different pariah block modules cultivate the boss' abilities. Modules like Kadence Blocks, Spectra (early Ridiculous Addons for Gutenberg), and Stackable add advanced blocks for things like looking over tables, beginning clocks, and picture records, and breathing in new life into parts. These blocks go past key substance creation, enabling you to join dexterous and overwhelming parts that overhaul client experience.

Presenting these block modules outfits you with extra inventive decisions as well as killing the fundamentals for discrete modules for every convenience. For example, rather than presenting a substitute module for assessing tables, you could present a complete block module that consolidates different versatile block types.

Using Full Site Editing (FSE) Capabilities with Gutenberg

With the approaching of Full Site development (FSE), Gutenberg has produced using a substance boss to a complete site-building instrument. FSE licenses clients to design headers, footers, and other setup parts clearly inside Gutenberg. This approach enables you to change your entire site plan from a singular connection point, staying aware of consistency without requiring a distant page creator. FSE is particularly useful for clients who need a lightweight, fast-stacking site.

FSE limits change by subject, so to utilize this part, ensure that you're using a subject that stays aware of FSE, for instance, Twenty 21 or a near-block-based subject. As frightening subjects take on FSE similitude, Gutenberg's real end concerning full-webpage page customization will continue to make, inciting it a solid decision for site page owners who without a second thought immediately jump all over the chance to keep all plan parts inside the WordPress focus.

Maximizing Gutenberg for a Professional Finish

Regulating the Gutenberg administrator outfits you with the instruments to make clean, fit substances without relying strongly on external modules or custom code. From its wide decision of focus blocks to state-of-the-art far-off decisions and Full Site page changes, Gutenberg offers serious strong regions for an up of instruments for anyone expecting to make present-day WordPress areas. By researching these components, you can streamline your substance creation process, raise the visual charm of your site, and gather plans that are both valuable and fulfilling.

5.2 Using Page Builders: Elementor, Divi, and More

For clients hoping to go past Gutenberg's local handiness, page makers like Elementor, Divi, and Beaver Specialist give progressed customization limits and visual course of action gadgets that improve on complex intends to accomplish. These page makers offer chipped-away-at interfaces, broad game plan highlights, and coordinated plans, permitting clients to make proficient objections without coding information. This part inspects the benefits, great highlights, and best showings of these striking page engineers.

The Advantages of Using Page Builders

Page producers give a more energetic and flexible plan experience veered from the standard WordPress chief. They offer boundless control over each page's arrangement, style, and handiness, empowering clients to make enamoring complaints particularly intended for their particular targets. For example, a business site can beyond a shadow of a doubt consolidate interesting parts like stimulated headers, parallax researching, and custom footers with insignificant exertion.

Page creators also give responsive game plan instruments, and that induces you can change how each page looks on changed contraptions. This adaptability is pivotal for making objections that are improved for both work areas and minimal clients, a fundamental part in 2025 as adaptable looking at keeps on overwhelming.

Elementor: Extensive Design Freedom and Rich Widget Library

Elementor is one of the most famous WordPress page makers because of its far-reaching contraption library, incessant front-end changing, and adaptable plan choices. With a wide gathering of coordinated associations and gadgets —, for example, picture merry-go-rounds, move bits, and acknowledgment sliders — Elementor awards clients to make shocking pages without requiring plan limits. In addition, it's not unexpected to deal with interface works on it for learners to begin making immediately.

Past its default gadgets, Elementor's Virtuoso variety presents progressed highlights, for example, pop-ups, plans, and improvement impacts, which can add dynamism to a site. Advancement impacts, for instance, award clients to add liveliness that triggers as guests scroll, causing them to see key substance parts. Elementor additionally keeps up with outsider trade-offs, so clients can foster its support with additional things like Silly Addons for Elementor and Crocoblock, which give additional plan parts.

Divi: Real-Time Editing and Customization Versatility

Divi is one more driving page maker known for its consistent, front-end adjusting limits. With Divi, clients can fabricate and alter their pages straightforwardly toward the front, seeing changes immediately. Divi's visual manager is standard, making it open to clients with no coding experience. It offers an expansive collection of arrangement contraptions, including custom CSS control, improvement impacts, and split testing, which allows clients to redesign plans and content for the most significant obligation.

Divi stands isolated for its general course of action choices, which let clients stay mindful of plan consistency across a whole site. For instance, a style applied to a button or header block can be for the most part set, guaranteeing steady styling across pages. Besides, Divi offers a basic library of coordinated plans, seeking after it an unprecedented decision for clients who like in any case plans and a brief time frame later re-attempt.

Beaver Builder: Simplicity and Flexibility for Developers and Non-Developers

Beaver Creator offers an equilibrium between straightforwardness and adaptability, making it famous with both vague clients and originators who need more basic command over their site's code. Beaver Maker's disengaged game plan framework awards clients to make hand creates utilizing lines, fragments, and modules for things like text, pictures, and plans. The creator's ideal code guarantees quick stacking speeds, which is productive for districts where execution is on an extremely essential level.

One of Beaver Maker's big enchilada parts is its comparability with other WordPress subjects and modules, which endpoints expected clashes. It besides offers a decent strategy of fashioner warm contraptions, similar to custom CSS and JavaScript fields for individual modules, making it more straightforward to apply custom styling or add novel comfort. Beaver Planner's adaptability licenses progressed clients to fit the experience to their necessities while as of now giving an unquestionable course of action cycle to young people.

Choosing the Right Page Builder for Your Needs

Each page engineer has extraordinary attributes, and picking the right one relies on your particular necessities, capacity level, and undertaking targets. Elementor is ideally suited for individuals who need to plan an entryway and enlistment to a tremendous contraption library, particularly if adding visual parts like turns of events and pop-ups is basic. Divi is unmistakably appropriate for clients who revolve around steady altering and critical level game plan choices, particularly expecting that they need by and large course of action control. Beaver Producer is reasonable for clients who worth clean code, closeness, and a quick plan process.

For adolescents, Elementor might be the most immediate regardless because of its easy-to-use interface and the wide assets open locally. In any case, assuming significant length adaptability and consent to maker mechanical gatherings are fundamental, Beaver Architect may be the better decision. For people who mean to make various locales with captivating stepping needs, Divi's general settings give the contraptions to accomplish a reliable tasteful.

Best Practices for Using Page Builders Effectively

To benefit from a page engineer, based on making perfect, practical associations. Try not to add an exorbitant number of contraptions and advancements, as these can restrain your site. Unendingly see your pages on work area, tablet, and versatile to guarantee your game plan is responsive and clear across all contraptions.

It's likewise fitting to utilize page creator additional things sparingly. However various additional things offer extra contraptions and elements, over-upsetting your site with an unnecessary number of additional things can incite apathetic stacking times and potential comparability issues. Stick to essential highlights, and dependably test new additional things in a straightening-out climate before doing them on your live site.

Leveraging Page Builders for a Unique Website

Page makers like Elementor, Divi, and Beaver Architect offer astounding assets for changing WordPress objections in 2025, permitting clients to make skilled, high-performing pages without depending upon custom code. By understanding the qualities of each page maker and utilizing them really, you can make a site that lines up with your plan vision, meets your handiness needs, and gives a sublime encounter to your guests.

5.3 Creating Dynamic and Responsive Content Blocks

In 2025, an essential piece of a high-performing site is the ability to show a dynamic and responsive substance that changes every open door to different screen sizes and client affiliations. Dynamic substance blocks grant site pages to offer adjusted data by changing substances considering the client's direction, area, or tendencies. These blocks other than ensure that plans remain beguiling and utilitarian across contraptions. This piece takes a gander at the systems, contraptions, and best practices for making dynamic, responsive substance blocks using WordPress and page engineers.

Understanding Dynamic Content in WordPress

Dynamic substance recommends parts on a site that are different considering various conditions. This could set showing different substances for returning clients versus new visitors or showing express blocks basically during unequivocal times or events. The dynamic substance increases client commitment by making the experience more basic and zeroed in on.

WordPress, when coexisted with page makers like Elementor and Divi, offers solid decisions for making dynamic substance. By consolidating modules like Unquestionable level Custom Fields (ACF) or Toolset, you can add custom fields to your posts and pages, allowing extraordinary data to be shown truly across your site. This part is particularly important for grumblings like internet-based business stores, adventure stages, or event protests where different clients need to see fluctuating sorts of content.

Creating Responsive Content Blocks with Flexibility in Design

Responsive substance blocks acclimate to different screen sizes to ensure that the affiliation, text, pictures, and blended media parts look astounding on any contraption. Building these blocks incorporates using adaptable networks, rates, and media requests instead of fixed perspectives. Latest page engineers, including Elementor, Divi, and Beaver Creator, go with worked-in responsive controls that grant you to anticipate workspace, tablet, and beneficial viewpoints independently.

For example, while putting together a substance block in Elementor, you can change padding, edges, text viewpoints, and, shockingly, observable quality for each contraption type. This level of customization is basic for keeping the substance clear and stunning across stages, as clients today access complaints from different contraptions, including PDAs, tablets, and workspace screens.

Utilizing Conditional Logic for Personalized Experiences

Contingent reasoning is a serious strong region for making the content much more important by showing unequivocal blocks contemplating client connection, locale, or page type. This value is generally around used in WordPress outlines and is before long becoming standard in page subject matter experts and modules. For example, with Elementor Star, you can set conditions for when certain parts or contraptions appear, for instance, showing a sublime development flag to clients who have visited your site on different events or showing region unequivocal offers.

Prohibitive reasoning furthermore deals with it to re-endeavor headers, footers, and wellspring of motivation areas. For example, a prosperity site can show wonderful designs to make a move for clients enthused about different development programs, similar to yoga or weightlifting. Executing prohibitive reasoning further makes client commitment by presenting content that is directly applicable to each visitor.

Animation and Interaction to Boost Engagement

Adding splendid parts, for instance, float influences, activities, and actuates, can make content blocks more energizing without overwhelming the client. In any case, these effects ought to be used circumspectly to avoid wreck and slow weight times. Most page producers grant you to add progressions and changes obviously through the boss. For instance, Elementor's improvement influences enable you to add fair activities to text or picture blocks, causing you to see key substance fragments without degrading the client experience.

While making liveliness, discovering some sort of benevolence between elegant charm and execution is colossal. Significant darkness-ins, slide-ins, or float influences are as oftentimes as possible sufficient to make content stand separated without compromising the site's speed. Avoid complex liveliness for moderate clients, as they can adversely influence stacking times and accommodation on extra humble screens.

Designing for Accessibility and User Experience

Responsive substance blocks should in this manner consider receptiveness to ensure a positive experience for all clients, joining those with frustrations. This induces using fitting heading structures, adding alt text to pictures, and ensuring that dexterous parts are successfully protected by the console. For example, while coordinating a block with tabs or accordions, ensure that these parts are open through the console course.

Plan contrast is correspondingly major, especially for clients with visual weaknesses. Guarantee that text is genuinely clear over establishment pictures or game plans, and consider using open text-based styles that are clear and clear on all screen sizes. By zeroing in on receptiveness in your responsive plans, you make a more thorough site that courses of action with a more critical social occasion.

Testing and Optimizing Responsive Content Blocks

Testing is strong to ensure that dynamic, responsive blocks are limited unequivocally on various contraptions and screen sizes. Right when a block is coordinated, see it on the workspace, tablet, and supportive points of view inside your page producer. Then, perform genuine testing on authentic contraptions to see any issues that evidently won't be discernible in the survey mode. Use program engineer mechanical social affairs to change parts relentlessly and refine the approach for different contraptions.

Disregarding contraption testing, truly research the page's stacking speed to ensure headways, pictures, and scripts are not causing inconveniences. Speed progress modules like WP Rocket or Smush can help with compacting pictures and direct hold, further working on the introduction of dynamic blocks.

Enhancing Engagement with Dynamic and Responsive Content

Making dynamic and responsive substance blocks is fundamental for building present-day, high-performing locales in 2025. By using instruments like ACF and page creators, setting contingent reasoning, and testing for contraption closeness, you can make a site that changes every open door to client needs while conveying a speaking with and open getting it.

5.4 Custom Code and Advanced Layouts

As WordPress keeps on making, site designers frequently look for more huge command over plans and plan parts to stand isolated from the opposition. Custom coding and certain level courses of action are fundamental contraptions in this pursuit, permitting you to accomplish amazing, apparently shocking plans that are arranged with unequivocal client needs. By uniting HTML, CSS, and JavaScript, you can make complex courses of action and fundamentally wise parts. This part hops into the potential gains of custom coding, frameworks for finishing best-in-class plans, and tips on keeping an improved, clear site.

When to Use Custom Code in WordPress

While WordPress and page planners like Elementor and Divi offer a wide course of action, several experiences require handiness or feel that beat worked in choices. Custom code awards you to break these limits and do remarkable plans, advancements, or natural highlights adjusted explicitly to your site's objectives. For instance, on the off chance that you truly need a custom float impact for thing pictures in an electronic business store or need to show client unequivocal information from an outside Programming association point, custom code can accomplish these outcomes much more profitably.

Prior to bobbing into coding, perceive your objectives and affirm that custom code is the best blueprint. For minor changes, for example, text style or grouping changes, you may essentially require head CSS. Regardless, for extra perplexing parts, for example, a completely patched-up course menu or dynamic information fields, certain level codes might be vital.

Structuring Advanced Layouts with HTML and CSS Grid

Building progressed plans start with orchestrating the HTML, as this plans the groundwork of your course of action. By utilizing semantic HTML5 marks (like <section>, <article>, and <aside>), you make sorts that are both available and Site improvement satisfying. Right when the advancement is set up, CSS Association and Flexbox offer strong ways to deal with organizing complex designs with precision.

CSS Organization is especially helpful for making lattice-based arrangements where parts change beneficially in lines and areas, ideal for portfolio pages, shows, or even complex spots of appearance. For example, you can set up a 12-segment association and control the size and position of parts with structure region endeavors, permitting you to change each part for a responsive game plan that changes impeccably to any screen size. Flexbox is essentially persuading for straight plans where parts are shown in movement or piece, for example, a course bar or a show merry-go-round.

Adding Interactivity with JavaScript

JavaScript plays a key part in adding information to cutting-edge plans, permitting you to make a genuinely beguiling and responsive client experience. For instance, JavaScript has some command over highlights like spring-up modals, sliding merry-go-rounds, or content that heaps constantly without requiring a full page enable. By inserting custom JavaScript into your WordPress site, you can offer clients an encounter that goes past static substance.

For regions utilizing jQuery, which is pre-bundled with WordPress, you can add regular parts with less code, as jQuery works on different common JavaScript tries. For example, finishing a "desire to top" button, separating show things, or making smooth examining liveliness should be possible effectively with jQuery.

Using Custom CSS for Fine-Tuning Styles

Custom CSS contemplates granular command over a site's look and feel, making it conceivable to change subtleties that may not be open through page fashioner settings. For instance, on the off chance that your page planner doesn't offer the specific disengaging, text-based style styles, or float impacts you need, adding custom CSS can assist with moving past these openings. CSS licenses you to set cautious edges, cushioning, cutoff points, and improvements, making a fundamentally clean plan.

One in number CSS part to investigate is the utilization of CSS factors, which let you portray reusable attributes, (for example, combinations or text perspectives) across the site. This keeps styles obvious as well as improves on it to do major developments by changing the components in a solitary district.

Implementing Conditional Logic for Dynamic Content

Restrictive thinking is a basic instrument for cutting-edge plans, as it awards you to show unequivocal substance considering client composed endeavors or conditions, for example, locale or contraption type. By getting JavaScript along with WordPress or utilizing modules like Obvious level Custom Fields (ACF), you can make exceptionally changed encounters. For instance, you can utilize restrictive thinking to show exceptional substance blocks to support clients, show various plans to take action for first-time guests, or even change plans thinking about the client's contraption.

This approach is particularly critical for web business complaints, support areas, or web journals with different gatherings, as it makes the experience more huge and draws in for every guest.

Optimizing Performance and Compatibility

While custom code and huge-level plans bring gigantic adaptability, they can comparably affect site execution on the off chance that not updated. Such incalculable custom things or critical CSS can actuate even more languid page load times, which could affect client experience and Site smoothing out. To facilitate this, use minification devices to pack your CSS and JavaScript records, and give insignificant things over to guarantee that focal substance stacks first.

Run-of-the-mill testing is essential to validate that custom code works magnificently across contraptions and ventures. Instruments like BrowserStack or Google Chrome Expert Contraptions permit you to reenact different gadgets and screen targets, guaranteeing a strong encounter. While sending new custom highlights, test them on adaptable, tablet, and work area perspectives to guarantee the game plan is responsive and instinctual parts work easily.

Maintaining Code Quality with Documentation and Version Control

Custom code can become testing to direct as a site develops, so it's essential to remain mindful of clear documentation and use form control. Recording each limit, style rule and affiliation guarantees that future updates or changes can be made effectively without disturbing the continuous site structure.

For complex activities, consider utilizing Git variety control to follow changes. In this manner, you can move back to past changes if fundamental, or truly team up with different experts without facing a challenge with information catastrophe. Utilizing a nearby improvement climate, such as Adjoining by Flywheel, permits you to test new custom codes and associations without influencing the live site.

Elevating Your Site with Custom Code and Advanced Layouts

Custom code and huge-level arrangements offer you the opportunity to make novel, high-performing objections that meet the particular necessities of your gathering. By utilizing HTML, CSS Framework, JavaScript, and restrictive thinking, you can plan normal, unprecedented setups that astonish clients. Try to focus on execution, test across contraptions, and record your work to guarantee that your customizations stay effective and flexible for quite a while. These systems will assist you with building a WordPress site that hangs out in 2025.

Chapter 6: Building an E-commerce Website with WooCommerce

In the high-level business focus of 2025, electronic business destinations have become more basic than at any time in recent memory, allowing associations to easily contact overall groups. WooCommerce, a solid and versatile WordPress module, offers generally what you need to make a first-class, totally helpful web-based store. In this part, we'll cover the essentials of building a web-based business website with WooCommerce, from foundation and plan to managing things, planning portion decisions, and further developing the shopping experience for your clients.

Setting Up WooCommerce on Your WordPress Site

To start collecting a web-based store, you first need to present WooCommerce, which ought to be conceivable clearly from the WordPress module document. Once started, WooCommerce dispatches a course of action wizard to guide you through major arrangements, including store region, cash settings, and cost decisions. This coordinated course of action chips away at the basic framework, helping you spread out the focal plane of your store quickly and definitively.

Right after completing the game plan, you'll see new menu decisions in the WordPress dashboard dedicated to administering various pieces of your store, similar to things, orders, and reports. Investigating these gadgets is huge, and necessary to keep a web-based business.

Adding and Organizing Products

The groundwork of any online business website is its thing list. WooCommerce grants you to add things autonomously, offering decisions to integrate point-by-point depictions, assessing, and pictures. For each thing, you can set credits like size, assortment, and class, simplifying it for clients to find definitively accurate things they need. WooCommerce moreover maintains mechanized things, downloadable substance, and enlistments, allowing you to upgrade your commitments if essential.

Orchestrating your things with classes and marks is major to additionally foster course and client experience. A particularly coordinated stock helps clients with finding things quickly as well as further develops your webpage's site smoothing out (Web enhancement) by making real pathways for web search instruments to record. Consider using clear, captivating characterizations and marks that reflect the key sorts of things you suggest to make the scrutinizing framework as instinctual as could truly be anticipated.

Configuring Payment and Shipping Options

Giving supportive portion and conveyance decisions is vital to offering a smooth shopping experience. WooCommerce maintains different portion entries, including PayPal, Stripe, and bank moves, which can be sorted out in the module's settings. Each portion entry goes with unequivocal features and trade costs, so essential to pick decisions line up with your business needs and fundamental vested party tendencies. For example, expecting your objective clients are around the world, offering different financial norms and portion methods is helpful.

Conveying decisions are likewise huge, especially expecting that your things are real items. WooCommerce gives strong transportation settings where you can portray conveying zones, set level rates, or engage consistent carrier calculations for dynamic conveyance costs. For associations working in various districts, setting up detached zones with uniquely crafted transportation decisions ensures that each client gets definite rates and movement times considering their region.

Designing a User-Friendly Shopping Experience

A productive electronic business site page is one that offers a predictable, interfacing with client experience. WooCommerce facilitates well with most WordPress subjects, yet using a WooCommerce-redesigned point can help you with achieving a specialist and straightforward arrangement even more capably. These subjects are attempted to highlight thing incorporates, smooth out course, and give an intuitive checkout process.

Consider adding principal online business parts, for instance, thing channels, search handiness, and a streamlined truck knowledge. Working on the visual appeal of your thing pages with magnificent pictures, video appearances, and client reviews can in like manner basically help client responsibility and change rates. The checkout connection should be essential, with irrelevant advances and a sensible wellspring of motivation, to decrease truck abandoning.

Utilizing Plugins and Extensions for Enhanced Functionality

WooCommerce offers a rich climate of modules and developments that engage you to add advanced components to your store. Expansions, for instance, WooCommerce Participations grant you to make continuing charging for enrollment based things, while WooCommerce Arrangements permits you to offer bookable organizations directly from your site. There are moreover instruments for administering stock, making tweaked discount codes, and adding live visit support.

One key module to consider is a client relationship the chiefs (CRM) joining, which grants you to follow client direct, segment groups, and put forth assigned advancing attempts. These instruments help you with redoing the shopping experience, build client commitment, and drive reiterate bargains. Regardless, be cautious while adding modules, as too many can tone down your site and confound upkeep.

Managing Orders and Customer Service

At the point when your WooCommerce store is going, directing requests gainfully transforms into a need. WooCommerce gives a solicitation the leaders system where you can follow what is going on with each solicitation, update stock, and talk with clients concerning their purchases. The dashboard shows each solicitation's nuances, for instance, things purchased, client information, and conveyance status, simplifying it to process and fulfill orders unequivocally.

Client support is another essential piece of running an online store. Responsive correspondence, clear product trades, and ideal updates can out and out influence buyer faithfulness and upkeep. WooCommerce integrates with email providers to automate client sees, including demand assertions and transportation invigorates. Executing a live visit or support labeling system can moreover update client care, especially if you are managing a high volume of solicitations.

Monitoring Store Performance and Analytics

Checking your store's show is major for getting a handle on client lead and further fostering your web business frameworks. WooCommerce offers worked in covers arrangements, pay, and thing execution, which can be gotten to clearly from the dashboard. For additional created assessment, think about planning Google Examination or using WooCommerce-unequivocal mechanical assemblies to follow changes, site hits, and client adventures.

Examination data can give huge encounters, for instance, perceiving your top of the line things, following client acquiring channels, and including areas of progress. By exploring these estimations reliably, you can refine your advancing undertakings, change assessing frameworks, and seek after data driven decisions that drive improvement.

Scaling Your Store as Your Business Grows

As your business develops, your online business site ought to be good for dealing with extended traffic, greater inventories, and more marvelous trades. WooCommerce is significantly versatile and maintains additional compromises and customizations that license your store to foster nearby your business. For example, if your thing stock develops, consider doing state of the art search channels, improved stacking methodologies, and a faster working with reply for stay aware of ideal execution.

At this stage, you may moreover have to place assets into advancing robotization, for instance, abandoned truck recovery messages or altered thing ideas, to help changes. Additionally, regularly reviving your modules, security settings, and fortifications is urgent for keep your store secure and totally down to earth as it creates.

Launching and Growing a Successful WooCommerce Store

Building an electronic business website with WooCommerce gives an adaptable and solid stage for business visionaries wanting to sell things on the web. From setting up portion and transportation decisions to arranging an associating with retail veneer and checking execution, each step adds to a fair electronic store that can attract, attract, and hold clients. By utilizing WooCommerce's expansive features and remaining flexible to creating on the web business designs, you can make a useful and adaptable business that twists in 2025's merciless modernized business community.

In the general business focal point of 2025, electronic business objections have become more fundamental than any time in late memory, permitting relationship to contact by and large gatherings without any problem. WooCommerce, a strong and flexible WordPress module, offers commonly that you want to make a five star, absolutely supportive online store. In this part, we'll cover the basics of building an online business site with WooCommerce, from establishment and plan to overseeing things, arranging segment choices, and further fostering the shopping experience for your clients.

6.1 Setting Up WooCommerce for Online Sales

Setting up WooCommerce for online game plans is a fundamental stage in changing your WordPress site into a sober-minded electronic business stage. This cycle incorporates arranging WooCommerce settings, depicting thing and part choices, and further fostering the store plan for a consistent client experience. Whether you're delivering off another online store or incorporating electronic business limits into a continuous webpage, WooCommerce gives the adaptability and parts expected to truly keep up with your electronic business.

Installing WooCommerce on WordPress

To start, WooCommerce should be introduced on your WordPress site. This should be possible truly by exploring the Modules segment in your WordPress dashboard, picking "Add New," and looking for "WooCommerce." When found, click "Present As of now" and a brief time frame later "Request." After beginning, WooCommerce will start a blueprint wizard that strolls you through essential game plans, including store subtleties, cash settings, and thing types. Finishing these techniques will fan out the center improvement of your web business store.

The WooCommerce course of action wizard permits you to pick suggested modules and elements, such as WooCommerce Divides or modernized charge estimation that can in addition work on your store's accommodation. After the secret arrangement, you'll advance toward the WooCommerce dashboard and all of the primary mechanical gatherings to begin fabricating your internet-based store.

Configuring Basic Store Settings

The subsequent stage consolidates coordinating your store's overall settings. In the WooCommerce settings menu, you'll track down choices to depict your store's region, selling districts, and cash propensities. For generally speaking stores, connecting with various monetary rules and setting sensible transportation zones can foster your market reach, obliging a general client base.

WooCommerce likewise offers command over charge settings, permitting you to arrange for whether costs are shown exhaustive or restrictive of commitment, and it can in this manner cycle charges thinking about client locales if the robotized charge highlight is empowered. Arranging these settings near the beginning guarantees a smooth checkout process for clients and consistency with neighboring commitment rules.

Adding Products to Your Store

Adding things is a huge piece of setting up WooCommerce. In the WordPress dashboard, examine Things and snap "Add New" to begin introducing things available to be purchased. Everything page gives fields to enter focal subtleties like thing name, depiction, cost, and SKU (stock keeping unit) for stock following. WooCommerce awards you to move critical standard pictures for everything, which manages the visual appeal of your store and lifts client obligation.

WooCommerce additionally keeps up with various thing types, including authentic things, advanced downloads, accumulated things, and variable things (things with different combinations like size or variety). Picking the proper thing type for everything guarantees clients have a smooth buying experience re-tried to their necessities. Extra settings like stock association, moving classes, and related thing contemplations can also be expected for an even more surprising store.

Configuring Payment Options

Offering a degree of peace strategies is significant to giving a steady shopping experience. WooCommerce keeps up with various part areas, including PayPal, Stripe, and WooCommerce Bits, which can be endorsed in the Segment locale under WooCommerce settings. Each piece entryway has unequivocal arrangement basics, and WooCommerce gives clear headings to direct you through accomplice your store to your inclined toward segment supplier.

For a smooth checkout experience, plan your part settings to perceive different choices if conceivable, as clients regard adaptability in segment systems. For by and large exchanges, guarantee your piece supplier keeps up with different cash-related standards, which can make your store more open to a general gathering.

Setting Up Shipping Options

Assuming your store sells genuine articles, it is imperative to set up transportation choices. WooCommerce licenses you to depict conveying zones, which are land locales where express transportation methods and rates apply. You can set up various zones to cover various regions, giving changed rates to neighborhoods and generally speaking clients.

WooCommerce additionally offers to convey choices like free movement, level rate, and nearby pickup. For cutting-edge needs, you ought to contemplate coordinating distant movement modules to offer nonstop transportation rates from transporters like USPS, FedEx, and DHL. Arranging exact transport settings fabricates client trust and guarantees a reasonable, clear checkout process.

Customizing Your Store's Appearance

With WooCommerce introduced, you can change the look and feel of your store to concur with your image character. Different WordPress subjects are WooCommerce-commonsense, permitting you to make an enthralling client standing up to outside without compromising accommodation. Pick a subject that features things, in all honesty, and offers versatile choices for tones, text styles, and plans.

Inside WooCommerce, you can comparably change the presence of thing pages, truck plans, and checkout pages. WooCommerce blocks are open for Gutenberg, drawing in you to add unequivocal parts like thing grids or checkout plans to various districts of your site. Making solid areas for an enchanting arrangement improves on it for clients to research and shop on your site.

Testing and Launching Your WooCommerce Store

Going before delivery off your store, serious testing is major to guarantee all parts are limited conveniently. Begin by adding test things and playing out a test buy to certify that checkout, piece, and movement settings fill in precisely true to form. Testing additionally permits you to perceive and conclude potential issues that could disturb the client experience.

Exactly when you're certain that your store works without issues, you're prepared to send off. Report your store's opening through virtual redirection, email showing, or progressions to drive fundamental traffic. Dependably update and upgrade your WooCommerce settings as you accumulate investigation and evaluation, assisting your store with adapting to client needs and increment can hope for a truly significant time frame.

Preparing for Success in E-commerce

Setting up WooCommerce for online plans outfits your site with the devices and highlights expected to flourish in the electronic business scene. By arranging center settings, adding things, and offering flexible piece and transport choices, you make an anticipated shopping experience that meets client doubts. With WooCommerce's versatility, your store can scale as your business makes, making it a critical early phase for maintained web business progress in 2025 no doubt.

6.2 Product Management: Adding, Editing, and Organizing Products

Overseeing things in WooCommerce is essential for maintaining an easy-to-use online store. The bosses integrate adding new items, restoring existing ones, and sorting out things to additionally foster client satisfaction. Understanding these parts assists you with making an expert store that is not difficult to shop from and advances deals.

Adding New Products

To add something else, go to the "Things" district in your WordPress dashboard and click "Add New." Here, you'll enter head data, such as the thing name, depiction, and short description, which appear on item postings and overviews. The long description ought to provide clear data to assist clients with making sense of the item's parts, advantages, and use cases.

Then, set a thing picture to address the thing and add a grandstand of extra photographs if imperative. Pictures are significant solid areas for an instrument, so fantastic visuals might from an overall perspective at any point help clients with interesting. WooCommerce besides gives fields to enter the thing's cost and a "deal cost" for limited things. Guarantee the thing's title, depiction, and pictures line up with your image to make a firm shopping experience.

Configuring Product Data: Types, Inventory, and Attributes

WooCommerce keeps up with different thing types, including Principal, Gathered, Outside/Accomplice, and Variable things. Something fundamental is a solitary thing without any choices, while something gathered awards you to sell a heap of related things together. Outside things partner with one more site for checkout, reasonable for part marketing specialists. Variable things, which offer choices like sizes or tones, let clients pick arrangements thinking about their propensities.

For everything, plan the stock settings under the "Stock" tab. You can empower the stock association, set the stock aggregate, and pick assuming that deferments are permitted. WooCommerce regularly tracks stock as courses of action happen, assisting you with remaining mindful of accurate stock levels and impeding overselling. In the "Attributes" tab, add any credits like size, combination, or material, which can upgrade separating and thing relationship toward the front.

Editing Product Details

Thing subtleties could require occasional updates to reflect changes in accessibility, regarding, or portrayals. To adjust something continuous, go to the "Things" area, find what you need to alter, and click "Change." Here, you can change any data, like regard, depiction, or thing pictures, and update stock levels or thing credits.

While stimulating a thing, consider the Website smoothing out prescribed procedures to work on its perceptible quality on web search gadgets. Ensure what title is important, review watchwords for depictions, and update what URL slug is key. By remaining mindful of resuscitated and definite thing data, you outfit clients with clear assumptions and a beautiful shopping experience.

Organizing Products with Categories and Tags

Groupings and imprints expect a focal part in coordinating your WooCommerce store, making it more straightforward for clients to find what they're searching for. Classes address general groupings of things, for example, "Apparel" or "Contraptions," while marks are more unambiguous names that get one-of-a-kind bits of the things, similar to "summer wear" or "waterproof."

To set up portrayals, go to "Products" > "Categories" in the dashboard. Here, you can make parent classes, and subcategories, and add pictures for each gathering. Dispatching things to classes is a fit strategy for planning clients and advance examining. Names can be added straightforwardly inside everything's changing page and are significant for extra sifting choices. Utilize a mix of classes and names to moreover cultivate course and expansion thing discoverability.

Using Product Variations for Flexible Options

For things that come in different choices, for example, clothing with various sizes or collections, WooCommerce's variable thing highlight licenses you to add these arrangements. Inside a thing page, select the "Thing Information" section and pick "Variable Thing" as the sort. Under the "Characteristics" tab, add credits like size and variety, and sometimes later lock in "Utilized for collections."

Then, go to the "Varieties" tab and snap "Make Groupings from All Credits." WooCommerce will make every under-the-sun mix, and you can change every arrangement with its own cost, picture, SKU, and stock level. This flexibility connects with clients to pick their leaned toward choices on something solitary page, further fostering their shopping experience and lessening page wreck.

Product Sorting and Display Customization

WooCommerce offers various ways to deal with controlling how things are shown in your store. You can set a default coordinating choice under "Change" > "WooCommerce" > "Product Catalog," picking between progressive sales, regularity, commonplace rating, most recent things, or custom getting sorted out. Custom arranging grants you truly to reorder things in the dashboard by pulling them up or down in the thing list.

Plus, WooCommerce-compatible themes occasionally coordinate choices for re-having a go at thing show, for example, framework or outline sees, picture sizes, and "fast view" buttons. Two or three focuses give contraptions that draw in included things shows, blockbusters, or unequivocal class features. Fitting the coordinating and showing of your things helps guide clients' regard for included or outstanding things, supporting the probability of game plans.

Managing Inventory and Stock Status

The sensible stock association is fundamental for keeping a smooth activity, particularly as things totals change long haul. WooCommerce's stock association devices permit you to follow stock levels, get alerts for low-stock things, and etch things as "In Stock," "Out of Stock," or "Backorder." In the WooCommerce settings under the "Things" tab, you can set general choices for low stock and difficult-to-reach observations.

For everything, utilize the "Inventory" tab to conclude stock aggregate and close whether IOUs are permitted. This tab additionally remembers amazing open doors for individual stock associations for thing collections, for example, following stock per grouping or size. By remaining mindful of cautious stock data, you take the necessary steps not to confound clients with shut-off things and smooth out request satisfaction.

Efficient Product Management

Competent thing the bosses is major to running a useful WooCommerce store. From adding new things to sorting out and restoring them, each step keeps a smoothed-out shopping experience for clients. By including WooCommerce's vivacious instruments for thing types, arrangements, and stock control, you can keep a coordinated store that strengthens deals, guarantees cautious thing transparency, and lines up with client notions.

6.3 Payment Gateways, Shipping, and Taxes

Setting up payment gateways, shipping options, and tax rates is crucial for giving a reliable checkout experience in WooCommerce. These parts structure the underpinning of your store's handiness, ensuring that clients can make purchases unhesitatingly, get precise conveyance checks, and settle the right appraisals. All of these plans impact the buyer's understanding, affecting their decision to complete trades and developing confidence in your store.

Choosing and Configuring Payment Gateways

Payment gateways are the systems that cycle charge card portions and other electronic portion techniques in WooCommerce. To set up portion entryways, investigate "WooCommerce" > "Settings" > "Portions" in the dashboard. WooCommerce maintains notable entrances like PayPal, Stripe, Square, and Authorize.net, allowing clients to pick a portion decision that suits them best. Picking strong entryways ensures a safeguarded trade process, which builds trustworthiness and endows clients.

Each entry offers intriguing benefits, so think about factors, for instance, trade charges maintained financial norms, and similitude with your client base. For instance, PayPal is for the most part seen and trusted, while Stripe offers a smooth Mastercard portion insight. WooCommerce in like manner engages compromise with adjacent portion entryways for express countries, developing your range to overall clients. Whenever you've picked an entry, plan its settings inside WooCommerce by entering the basic Programming point of interaction keys and seller nuances, then, test the entryway to promise it processes portions without any problem.

Setting Up Shipping Options

Conveying plan in WooCommerce consolidates portraying moving zones, strategies, and rates. Conveying zones license you to demonstrate moving procedures and rates considering client regions, giving you the versatility to change conveying decisions for various locales. To fire setting up transportation, go to "WooCommerce" > "Settings" > "Conveyance." Here, you'll make conveying zones for the areas you serve, as local, around the world, or unequivocal regions inside a country.

For every conveyance zone, add shipping procedures like level rate, free transportation, or neighborhood pickup. Level rate allows an anticipated cost, while free conveyance can be planned as a restricted time decision. You may in like manner offer nonstop transportation rates accepting that using blends in with carriers like USPS, FedEx, or DHL, which find out conveying costs considering weight, viewpoints, and goals. Each technique can be changed as per different transportation requirements, similar to commitment helped or standard movement decisions.

WooCommerce also maintains modules that integrate with different carriers to give dynamic transportation rates and checks, robotizing conveying processes, and updating purchaser steadfastness. By orchestrating clear and definite conveyance decisions, you help clients understand the transportation costs, diminishing truck give up in view of surprising charges.

Configuring Tax Rates for Your Store

Setting up charges is major to agree to regional evaluation guidelines and thwart unexpected charges for clients. WooCommerce offers a reasonable obligation plan process that grants you to portray charge rates considering your store's region and your clients' conveyance addresses. To enable charges, go to "WooCommerce" > "Settings" > "General," and really investigate the holder to engage charges. This will add a "Cost" tab to your settings menu.

Inside the "Cost" tab, plan charge settings, for instance, showing costs thorough or prohibitive of evaluation, changing charge at the subtotal level, and choosing obligation calculation considering conveyance or charging addresses. WooCommerce permits you to set up various cost rates, which can be applied considering the region. For example, you could require different rates for local and overall clients or variable rates inside a singular country.

You can manage these cost rates under "Standard Rates," "Lessened Rate Rates," and "Zero Rate Rates" inside the "Evaluation" settings. Enter the specific rates applicable to each area, and WooCommerce will normally apply them at checkout. If charge guidelines change, it's essential to update these rates to stay aware of consistency and avoid issues with client sales.

Enabling Automated Tax Calculation

For vendors who need to chip away at charge calculations, WooCommerce gives blend mechanized charge game plans like WooCommerce Obligation or untouchable modules like Avalara or TaxJar. These gadgets thus figure out charges considering the latest appraisal rules and client regions, ensuring consistency and saving time on manual obligation game plans. Robotized courses of action are especially useful for stores serving various regions, where appraisal rates vacillate comprehensively.

Mechanized charge courses of action update charge rates consistently, changing considering close-by guidelines and changes. This ensures precision in control assessments, giving clients a direct viewpoint on the costs they'll be paying and facilitating vendors from progressive updates. In any case, note that a few modules could have related costs or participation charges, so evaluate whether robotized charge assessment is major for your store considering bargains volume and multifaceted nature.

Testing Payment, Shipping, and Tax Settings

Resulting in orchestrating portion sections, shipping decisions, and cost rates, testing the checkout cycle is critical. Put in test demands using different portion methodologies, conveying complaints, and client profiles to avow that obligations and conveyance charges apply precisely. Use sandbox conditions given by portion entrances like PayPal and Stripe to deal with test trades without authentic portions.

Testing licenses you to distinguish issues in your checkout cycle, for instance, mixed-up charge rates, unexpected transportation expenses, or bombarded trades. Standard testing, especially after revives or module changes, ensures that clients participate in a smooth and definite checkout experience. Explore any botches in a flash and suggest WooCommerce documentation or sponsorship expecting that you experience complex issues.

Providing a Seamless Checkout Experience

Setting up portion entries, shipping decisions, and costs is a crucial piece of making a simple-to-utilize WooCommerce store. By offering secure portion methodologies, clear transportation rates, and careful cost assessments, you overhaul client conviction and invigorate changes. Carefully planning these parts helps you with consenting to legal essentials as well as gives a direct shopping experience that cuts off points of truck abandoning and further creates purchaser reliability.

Setting up segment entrances, conveying choices, and commitment rates is urgent for giving a solid checkout experience in WooCommerce. These parts structure the support of your store's handiness, guaranteeing that clients can make buys unhesitatingly, get exact transport checks, and settle the right examinations. These plans influence the purchaser's grasping, influencing their choice to finish exchanges and creating trust in your store.

6.4 Managing Orders, Customers, and Reports

Successfully controlling requests, clients, and reports in WooCommerce is basic for running a smooth, adaptable web business. These parts assist you with following exchanges, give remarkable client care, and pursue information-driven choices that add to progression. WooCommerce offers essential assets for request satisfaction, client the board, and evaluation, all of which expect a segment in conveying a smoothed-out shopping experience and managing your store's show.

Processing and Fulfilling Orders

Request the board start with following and satisfying client puts together conveniently. In WooCommerce, every request is given a status, for example, "Looming," "Managing," "On Hold," "Finished," or "Dropped." To see and control orders, go to "WooCommerce" >

"Orders" in the dashboard, where you can see a design of all sales and redirect them thinking about status or date.

For every sale, WooCommerce gives focal subtleties, including request things, client data, charging and moving addresses, and notes. From this view, you can additionally fortify interest conditions with reflected progress. For instance, set a request to "Dealing with" whenever the segment is affirmed and "Wrapped up" when the thing is sent. Restoring conditions with clients informed about their sales' association and licenses you to follow satisfaction interminably.

WooCommerce in addition empowers fractional satisfaction, permitting you to take a look at individual things as moved on the off chance that they're sent unreservedly. For immense augmentation stores, consider combining request the board modules that robotize stock following, make moving engravings, and send clients modernized advice about request observes. These contraptions smooth out endeavors and foil delays, in the end further creating purchaser immovability.

Communicating with Customers

Directing client straightforwardness is basic for building trust and empowering rehash business. WooCommerce's plan-the-board devices incorporate choices to email clients ordinarily when certain requesting status changes happen. For instance, when a request is independent of "Finished," WooCommerce can send a demand email with transportation subtleties. These messages can be changed in "WooCommerce" > "Settings" > "Messages," permitting you to stamp correspondences with your logo, combinations, and enlightening.

Despite robotized messages, you can add manual notes to sales, either as inner notes for accomplices or as client notes discernible to the purchaser. Client notes are particularly significant assuming that there are changes to the request, for example, yields in movement or extra data anticipated from the client. This straightforwardness decreases missteps and accumulates affection, showing clients that you're based on keeping them informed.

WooCommerce similarly gives devices to client relationships with the pioneers (CRM) through different modules. CRMs permit you to follow client affiliations, record propensities, and alter future correspondences by thinking about past buys. This approach invigorates an unflinching client base by making a re-tried shopping experience, where clients feel respected and comprehended.

Utilizing Reports and Analytics

Reports and appraisal are principal for following your store's presentation, figuring out client leads, and seeing open entrances for development. WooCommerce merges worked in uncovering mechanical congregations available under "WooCommerce" > "Reports." Here, you can audit information on deals, orders, client action, and stock levels.

Deals reports are among the fundamental experiences, as they give data on complete game plans, limits, net courses of action, and regular standard compensation. Request reports assist you with seeing how much demands, request worth, and status breakdown, outfitting you with a conspicuous image of your game plans pipeline. With these experiences, you can figure out which things are top transporters, see times of high plan action, and pursue informed stock choices.

For extra appraisal, consider coordinating Google Assessment or WooCommerce-unequivocal assessment modules that suggest further snippets of data into client leads, reference sources, and client financial aspects. These instruments permit you to follow change rates, screen client journeys and appreciate where clients drop off during the shopping system. By isolating this information, you can update displaying attempts, further cultivate web designing, and fashioner thing responsibilities to fulfill client needs.

Managing Customer Accounts

Client account the board is one more significant piece of WooCommerce that further makes client experience. WooCommerce licenses clients to make accounts, which works on the checkout correspondence for repeat buys. To empower record creation, go to "WooCommerce" > "Settings" > "Records and Protection," where you can change account settings, including visitor checkout choices and security moves close.

Client accounts store data like sales history, charging and conveying addresses, and saved segment techniques. Clients can get to their sales history and track dynamic orders straightforwardly, decreasing the essential for help demands. Additionally, client accounts support dedication programs and adjusted showing structures, as you can isolate clients thinking about obtaining history or rehash of solicitations.

Directing client accounts in this way combines managing advantages, cutoff points, and revocations. WooCommerce's development of the pioneer's framework works on it as far as possible straightforwardly from the dashboard, either for full or halfway totals. By offering adaptable item exchanges and able cutoff points, you show clients that you base on their fulfillment, which is major for building brand resolute quality.

Leveraging Automation and Integrations

Mechanization could from an overall perspective at any point decline the commitment related to coordinating solicitations, client affiliations, and uncovering. WooCommerce incorporates a huge number of instruments, for example, email propelling stages, CRMs, and assessment plans, permitting you to robotize tries like coming about messages, stock level updates, and execution revealing.

For example, email mechanization stages like MailChimp or Klaviyo can be connected with WooCommerce to send allowed crusades considering client leads. Mechanized missions can help clients with recalling deserted trucks, advance-related things, or idea endpoints to assist with repeating buys. Mechanizing these undertakings saves time and guarantees a strong obligation with your client base.

Request the board modules in addition give stock following and tweaked reordering limits, which block stockouts and keep something expected supply. Many stores depend upon ERP (Endeavor Asset Sorting out) contraptions to change stock, control providers, and smooth out tasks across deals channels. By utilizing these blends, you guarantee that WooCommerce scales really as your business makes, remaining mindful of high help rules without requiring wide manual intercession.

Streamlining Operations for Success

Overseeing sales, clients, and reports successfully is vital to a successful WooCommerce store. By effectively managing orders, strong regions for creating affiliations, and utilizing information snippets of data, you fabricate a consistent shopping experience that draws in trust and rehash business. Arranging computerization instruments and outside associations further deals with these cycles, saving time for key courses. WooCommerce's liberal cutoff points allow you to deal with all bits of store the bosses in a single spot, guaranteeing that you're able to scale your business and convey exceptional client care.

Chapter 7: Optimizing for Speed, Security, and Performance

Guaranteeing a quick, secure, and high-performing WordPress site is key for a useful electronic presence, particularly as clients in 2025 anticipate consistent encounters. Further developing these parts can maintain your site's web document rankings, further cultivate client backing, and defend it from chances. In this part, we'll hop into ways to deal with additional creating site speed, fix security, and lift execution for a liberal WordPress site.

Understanding the Importance of Website Speed

Page speed obviously influences client experience and web record rankings, with quicker regions by and large arranging higher and holding guests longer. Focuses on showing that clients leave areas that anticipate that more than three seconds should stack, focusing on speed. Speed streamlining starts with picking a solid working supplier that offers quick servers and adaptable assets for overseeing traffic€ € floods.

Past working with, and taking care of is a basic speed-updating system. Holding quickly stores static varieties of your site, reducing the time it takes to stack pages to bring visitors back. Contraptions like WP Rocket and W3 Out and Out Hold further develop taking care of WordPress clients, and they go with direct strategy choices. By executing holding, you decline server trouble and endlessly out additional encourage page load times.

One more imperative piece of speed streamlining is picture pressure. Huge pictures can restrain stacking times, so squeezing them before moving can decrease chronicle sizes without compromising quality.

Modules like Smush and Imagify robotize this cooperation, permitting you to further develop pictures on the move and work on your site's show.

Enhancing Security: Protecting Your Site from Threats

With broadening network protection gambles, getting your WordPress site is a more significant need than at later. WordPress, being an exhaustively utilized stage, is a common target for designers; in this manner, it is non-simple to disprove to do essential security rehearses. Begin by picking a respectable security module like Wordfence or Sucuri, which gives highlights like firewall insurance, malware checking out, and login have a go at taking notes.

Drawing in SSL (Secure Associations Layer) is another fundamental security step. SSL scrambles information traded among clients and the site, protecting delicate data. Generally working with suppliers offers free SSL affirmations, which you can arrange through your control board. SSL-got locales comparably get an arranging lift on web crawlers, further making perceivable quality.

Dependably empowering WordPress concentration, subjects, and modules is major for security, as updates a large part of the time combine patches for newly found inadequacies. Set up altered stimulates if conceivable or screen your dashboard for alarms. Besides, conveying strong regions for out and restricting login attempts can impede unapproved access and animal power assaults, which are conventional dangers for WordPress protests.

Improving Performance with Database Optimization

The WordPress information base stores regularly your site's information, including posts, remarks, and module settings. Throughout a drawn-out time, instructive assortments can become extended with silly information, for example, changes, spam remarks, and vagabonds. Instructive assortment streamlining contraptions, such as WP-Improve or Critical level Educational assortment Cleaner, can assist with tidying up unused information and diminish enlightening assortment size, accomplishing prevalent execution.

Refreshing your enlightening record further creates speed as well as further makes site reliability by limiting the opportunity for educational assortment-related bungles. These gadgets consistently give mechanized cleaning plans, guaranteeing that your information base extra parts are improved without manual mediation. For more noteworthy regions, consider utilizing a serious information base server to oversee high-traffic loads and complex demands much more competently.

Leveraging Content Delivery Networks (CDNs) for Global Reach

A Substance Transport Affiliation (CDN) can quite furthermore cultivate site speed, especially for clients getting to your site from various locales. CDNs work by conveying duplicates of your site's substance across a general relationship of servers. Precisely when a client visits your site, the CDN serves content from the server nearest to their area, reducing laziness and accelerating load times.

Prestigious CDN suppliers like Cloudflare and StackPath unite really with WordPress, offering saving, security, and execution benefits. By utilizing a CDN, you accelerate fulfilled development as well as decline server load, and further encourage site uptime during traffic spikes. CDNs also add a layer of insurance by camouflaging your server's IP address, which can coordinate unambiguous sorts of assaults.

Minimizing Plugin and Script Usage

While modules add critical support to WordPress, extreme utilization of modules can actuate even more languid stacking times and stretch out weakness to security wagers. Decreasing how many modules on your site can assist with overhauling execution, particularly expecting you challenged person or kill modules with covering highlights. Assess the need for every module and mission for top-kind, multi-down-to-earth modules that can play out different undertakings.

JavaScript and CSS keep besides expect a part in site speed. Enormous or unoptimized things can defer page stacking, influencing the client experience. Minification contraptions, such as Autoptimize and WP Rocket, pack CSS and JavaScript records, discarding inconsequential spaces and remarks. These contraptions harden different CSS or JavaScript records into single reports, decreasing how many deals made to the server and further making page load times.

Monitoring and Testing Performance Regularly

Streamlining for speed, security, and execution is positively not a one-time process; it requires consistent seeing any changes. Mechanical congregations like Google PageSpeed Snippets of Data, GTmetrix, and Pingdom give wretched execution reports, featuring regions that need improvement. These instruments measure load time, give movement considerations, and allow you to isolate redesigns in the wake of executing changes.

Security checking is equivalently basic. Security modules consistently go with arranged settings that tell you of sketchy turn of events or inadequacies. Regular reaches and investigating assist with getting potential security wagers before they influence your site. Occasional reviews, driven month to month or quarterly, guarantee that your site stays in ideal condition and frustrate individual time or execution issues.

Balancing Speed, Security, and Functionality

In 2025, a high-performing WordPress site will change speed, security, and comfort. Improving speed through taking care of, picture pressure and CDN joining makes a smoother client experience, while security tries like SSL, commonplace updates, and firewalls safeguard your site from taking chances. At last, obvious checking and educational assortment improvement guarantee that your webpage stays mindful of extended execution, supporting areas of strength for an expert internet-based presence that can scale as your gathering makes. By following these embraced systems, you'll foster an expedient, secure, and adaptable WordPress site that fulfills the high assumptions of the ongoing clients.

7.1 Speed Optimization Techniques for 2025

As site guests expect quicker and smoother encounters than at later, speed improvement has changed into a key piece of site pioneers. A speedier page positions better on web crawlers as well as upgrades client fulfillment and backing. In this section, we will major areas of strength for cover streamlining procedures that can assist with guaranteeing your WordPress site is fast and responsive in 2025.

Leveraging Next-Generation Image Formats

In 2025, best-in-class picture game plans, for example, WebP and AVIF have changed into the norm for uncommon yet essentially squeezed pictures. These affiliations offer essential record size decreases stood apart from standard plans like JPEG and PNG, which is key for speed overhaul. By trading pictures over absolutely to WebP or AVIF, you diminish the information your clients need to download, speeding up page load times without compromising visual quality. Different modules, such as Smush and ShortPixel, ordinarily convert and advance pictures for you, guaranteeing a fruitful and smoothed-out process.

Utilizing Efficient Caching Mechanisms

Saving is one of the most astonishing rate improvement approaches for WordPress objections. Saving immediately stores duplicates of your site's information, diminishing the heap on your server and reducing inconvenience times for guests. Devices like WP Rocket, W3 Full-scale Store, and LiteSpeed Save make holding fundamental, offering a lone tick choice for both server-side and program saving. By holding pages, pictures, and records, you award returning clients to get to content quicker while working with server strain. Holding can correspondingly relax to versatile clients, it is equally rapid and consistent to guarantee advantageous investigating encounters.

Adopting Lazy Loading for Media Files

Lethargic stacking is a very front streamlining technique that deferrals stacking pictures and records until they enter the client's view. This approach diminishes the fundamental weight time since just toward the top substance loads when a client first gets to the page. WordPress at this point has suggested help for sluggish stacking pictures, and modules, for example, Slow Weight by WP Rocket relaxes this handiness to accounts and different media types. By applying sluggish stacking, your site turns out to be essentially lighter and more responsive, especially for media-significant pages.

Minimizing JavaScript and CSS Files

Gigantic or unoptimized JavaScript and CSS records can foment page speed by surrendering content conveying. Minification is a cycle that lessens record sizes by killing whitespace, remarks, and worthless code. Contraptions like Autoptimize and WP Rocket give minification and mix choices, which pack reports and assemble them into less demands. By confining and joining JavaScript and CSS, you decrease how much server demands, accomplishing speedier weight times and a smoother examining experience.

Implementing Content Delivery Networks (CDNs)

Taking into account general reach, Content Development Affiliations (CDNs) are major for fast execution in 2025. A CDN stores duplicates of your site's static resources across a relationship of geologically dissipated servers, lessening dormancy by giving bliss from the closest server to the client. Cloudflare, StackPath, and BunnyCDN are notable choices that capacity wonderfully with WordPress. By utilizing a CDN, you guarantee that your site stacks rapidly for clients all around the planet, making it particularly significant for regions with overall gatherings.

Taking Advantage of HTTP/3 Protocol

The HTTP/3 show has arisen as another norm, further making information move paces and security over past varieties. HTTP/3 presents the QUIC show, which totally decreases connection game-plan times and further improves page load speed. Different CDNs and working with suppliers, such as Cloudflare and Kinsta, support HTTP/3, permitting WordPress regions to profit from speedier stacking times and better security. Assuming you're working with a supplier that offers HTTP/3, drawing in it can accomplish perceptible execution redesigns.

Optimizing Database and Reducing Bloat

WordPress educational assortments accumulate unused information throughout a drawn-out time, including post updates, drifters, and spam remarks, which can restrain your site. Routinely cleaning and overhauling the educational assortment utilizing modules like WP-Improve or Huge level Instructive assortment Cleaner takes out paltry information and decreases enlightening record size. Furthermore, characterizing explicit limits on post alterations and dependably concentrating on your modules and subjects for unused parts can impede future educational record development, impelling quicker, more fruitful execution.

Using Server-Side Compression: GZIP and Brotli

Server-side strain endlessly diminishes the size of files sent from the server to the program, lessening inconvenience times. GZIP and Brotli are eminent pressure calculations that can decrease HTML, CSS, and JavaScript chronicles by up to 70%. Many web servers and working with suppliers eventually assist Brotli with constraining, which is more remarkable than GZIP, particularly when utilized close by CDNs. Connecting with these pressure procedures can accelerate the development of your site's substance to clients, giving a quick lift in execution.

Choosing a High-Performance Hosting Provider

Your working with the supplier plays a major part in site speed, as server reaction times straightforwardly influence load speed. Regulated WordPress working with suppliers, such as Kinsta, WP Motor, and SiteGround, offer explicit associations that advance for speed, dependability, and flexibility. Search for working with plans that give SSD putting away, fast PC processors, and a lot of server assets to help your site's necessities. A tremendous number of these hosts likewise solidify characteristics taking care of, CDNs, and SSL, which further upgrades speed and regular execution.

Ensuring Continuous Speed Optimization

The best method for overseeing speed updates in 2025 consolidates a mix of present-day procedures, from picture plan levels of progress to utilizing CDNs and taking on HTTP/3. Routinely seeing your site's speed utilizing instruments like Google PageSpeed Snippets of data, GTmetrix, and Pingdom awards you to perceive any regions for headway. Using finishing and refining these systems, you'll guarantee your WordPress site page conveys quick, unsurprising encounters for clients, actuating higher obligation, better web crawler rankings, and lastly, better headway on the web.

7.2 Security Best Practices to Protect Your Website

In 2025, with network assurance perils growing more complicated, getting your WordPress site is basic. Effective security endeavors protect sensitive client data as well as help with staying aware of your site's standing, thwart leisure time, and shield pay. In this part, we'll cover the latest security best practices to ensure your site is especially protected against typical shortcomings and anticipated attacks.

Keeping WordPress, Themes, and Plugins Updated

One of the most essential security practices is reliably invigorating WordPress focus, points, and modules. Various security shortcomings come from out-of-date programming, which software engineers exploit to gain admittance. The WordPress improvement neighborhood of the time releases updates to fix security flaws, making it fundamental to stay current. In your WordPress dashboard, you can engage in modified updates or set up admonitions to caution you when updates are free. By staying aware of revived programming, you prevent aggressors from exploiting known weaknesses.

Implementing Strong Passwords and User Access Management

Weak passwords are a regular purpose segment for software engineers, making it fundamental to use strong, novel passwords for all client accounts on your site. A strong mystery key consolidates a mix of promoted and lowercase letters, numbers, and pictures, and ideally should be something like 12 characters long. Secret word chairmen like LastPass or 1Password make it clearer to make and store complex passwords securely. Moreover, limit client access by giving out positions and assents carefully. Simply grant chief distinctions to clients who need them, diminishing the bet of unapproved access.

Enabling Two-Factor Authentication (2FA)

Two-factor confirmation (2FA) is a fruitful technique for improving login security by requiring an additional step past a mystery expression. With 2FA, clients ought to affirm their personality through a resulting procedure, like a code sent off their phone or a confirmation application like Google Authenticator. This extra layer of well-being makes it harder for software engineers to get to your site, whether or not they have the right mystery state. Modules like Wordfence and WP 2FA arrange explicit replies that deal with serious consequences regarding engaging 2FA on your WordPress site.

Using Secure Hosting and SSL Certificates

Picking a dependable, secure working with a provider is vital to protecting your site. Quality working with providers offers solid security features, including firewalls, interference acknowledgment, and malware-looking. Various providers similarly consolidate free Secure Connections Layer (SSL) supports, which scramble data moved between your site and clients. An SSL confirmation is central for security as well concerning client trust, as projects mark regions without SSL as "Not Secure." Assurance your working with the provider maintains these components to lay out solid areas for a point for site security.

Regularly Backing Up Your Website

Fortifications are fundamental to recovering your site if there should be an occurrence of a cyberattack or data hardship. A strong support system allows you to restore your site quickly without gigantic wiggle room time or data incident. Ideally, fortifications should be motorized and taken care of off-site, separate from your work with the provider. Modules like UpdraftPlus, BackupBuddy, and Jetpack offer booked fortifications and simplify them to restore your site if fundamental. Ordinary fortifications ensure that you can recover from security events with inconsequential interference.

Installing a WordPress Security Plugin

A total security module can evaluate your site for questionable activity and give protection against typical risks like monster force attacks and malware. WordPress security modules, such as Wordfence, Sucuri, and iThemes Security, offer various features, including malware-looking at, firewall confirmation, and progressing alerts. These modules successfully inspect your site, blocking malevolent IP areas and making you mindful of any shortcomings. By using a trusted security module, you overhaul your site's watchmen and make it harder for developers to enter.

Protecting the WordPress Admin Area

The WordPress head district is a fundamental goal for developers, so it is essential to safeguard it. One technique for getting this locale is by changing the default login URL from "/wp-overseer" to a custom URL. This diminishes the likelihood of creature power attacks zeroed in on the standard login page. Likewise, consider confining login tries to hinder repeated unapproved access attempts. Modules like Limit Login Attempts Reloaded help you with setting limits and lockout periods for failed logins, blocking software engineers from guessing passwords.

Using File Permissions and Disabling File Editing

Report assents control who can examine, form, and execute records on your server. Improper record assents can incite security shortcomings, especially accepting developers get adequately near sensitive reports. Set record approvals carefully, ideally using the assents 644 for reports and 755 for libraries. Likewise, handicap report modifying inside the WordPress dashboard by adding define('DISALLOW_FILE_EDIT', substantial); to your wp-config.php record. This keeps unapproved clients from changing records if they draw near enough to your dashboard.

Enforcing Regular Security Audits and Monitoring

Standard security surveys help with recognizing expected shortcomings before they're exploited. Audits incorporate looking over your site's course of action, access logs, and security settings to ensure everything is secure. WordPress security modules as often as possible integrate audit logs, which track changes to your site, for instance, login attempts and record changes. By reviewing these logs infrequently, you can recognize questionable activity and address potential risks. Consider arranging surveys month to month to stay aware of safety standards and catch issues early.

Staying Proactive with Security Measures

Security is a tenacious communication that requires watchfulness, as new risks emerge reliably. By following these endorsed methods — keeping your item revived, solid areas for executing controls, and using security modules — you make good insurance against likely attacks. Additionally, staying informed about WordPress security designs and proactively driving standard audits ensures that your site stays secure and strong for clients. Taking these steps now will shield your site's uprightness and reputation, giving both you and your visitors an internal sensation of amicability.

7.3 Implementing Caching, CDN, and Lazy Loading

Improving a site's exhibition is fundamental for upgrading client experience and decreasing burden times, the two of which are basic to Web optimization and guest maintenance. Three amazing assets for further developing site speed are reserving, content conveyance organizations (CDNs), and apathetic stacking. This segment gives experiences into every one of these devices and makes sense of how they cooperate to make a quick, effective site.

Understanding Caching and Its Benefits

Storing is one of the least difficult yet best ways of diminishing server load and further developing page load speeds. At the point when a guest gets to a site, the server needs to get information from the data set and render it each time the page is stacked. Storing saves a static form of regularly mentioned content, similar to HTML pages, pictures, and scripts, so the server doesn't have to recover it without any preparation on each visit.

There are two primary kinds of reserving: server-side and program-side storing. Server-side storing saves information on the server, so the site is conveyed quicker to clients. Program side reserving, then again, stores information on the client's gadget, so when they return to the site, their program can stack resources like pictures and CSS records from neighborhood capacity. This essentially lessens load times. Well-known WordPress reserving modules like W3 Complete Reserve and WP Super Store make carrying out storing direct, offering choices for altering what gets reserved and how lengthy it's put away.

Leveraging CDNs to Deliver Content Faster

A substance conveyance organization (CDN) is an organization of servers disseminated internationally to convey site content from the nearest server to the client. This fundamentally further develops load times for clients who are a long way from the beginning server, as the CDN stores duplicates of the site's resources —, for example, pictures, JavaScript records, and CSS documents — on different hubs all over the planet.

CDNs work by circulating substances across various servers, which speeds up conveyance as well as diminishes server load, and safeguards against traffic spikes. For WordPress clients, well-known CDN administrations like Cloudflare, StackPath, and Amazon CloudFront offer reconciliation with simple toutilize modules. With a CDN, clients visiting your site from various locales will encounter quicker load times, as the substance is conveyed from the closest server as opposed to the beginning. This approach is particularly gainful for media-weighty locales or those focusing on a worldwide crowd.

Implementing Lazy Loading for Optimized Resource Usage

Lethargic stacking is a method that concedes the stacking of unnecessary components on a page until they are required, normally when a client looks down to see them. Pictures, recordings, and installed content like iframes are normal components that advantage of sluggish stacking. By stacking these components just surprisingly, apathetic stacking decreases starting page load times and saves transfer speed, particularly for portable clients or those with restricted information plans.

In WordPress, lethargic stacking can be effortlessly empowered through modules like Smush or Apathetic Burden by WP Rocket. These modules permit you to alter apathetic stacking settings, picking which components ought to stack just when important. WordPress itself presented local apathetic stacking for pictures in ongoing adaptations, and that implies it's feasible to carry out this element without modules for straightforward picture taking care of. Apathetic stacking can be especially compelling for pages with various media components, like portfolios, sites, and displays, considering smooth looking over and quicker page conveyance.

Combining Caching, CDNs, and Lazy Loading for Optimal Results

Reserving, CDNs, and lethargic stacking each add to execution in one-of-a-kind ways, and when utilized together, they give a strong lift to site speed and client experience. Reserving limits the requirement for rehashed information recovery, CDNs carry content nearer to clients around the world, and languid stacking lessens asset utilization by just stacking noticeable components. Together, these strategies make a quick, proficient site that conveys content quickly and easily, regardless of the client's area or gadget.

The best methodology is to consolidate these devices with other speed improvement rehearses, similar to picture pressure and minifying CSS and JavaScript. Numerous WordPress execution modules, as WP Rocket and NitroPack, offer complete arrangements that consolidate storing, apathetic stacking, and CDN mix in one bundle, making it simpler to deal with these components.

Monitoring and Testing Your Site's Performance

In the wake of carrying out storing, CDNs, and lethargic stacking, consistently testing your site's presentation is critical. Apparatuses like Google PageSpeed Bits of Knowledge, GTmetrix, and Pingdom give bits of knowledge into what these advancements mean for load times and client experience. By assessing your site's speed and checking on unambiguous suggestions for development, you can distinguish any bottlenecks and tweak settings.

Execution testing additionally permits you to survey how well these devices cooperate. For example, some storing settings might struggle with CDN arrangements or certain sluggish stacking executions might influence picture quality. Testing assists you with making informed acclimations to boost the advantages of every strategy while guaranteeing a consistent encounter for clients.

Streamlining Performance for User Satisfaction and SEO

Executing storing, CDNs, and apathetic stacking is fundamental for improving your site's speed, which straightforwardly influences client fulfillment and web index rankings. These devices assist with overseeing server assets productively, diminish load times, and guarantee content arrives at clients rapidly. By joining these strategies and checking their viability, you can make a WordPress site that fulfills the needs of the present computerized scene, offering a quick and solid experience for clients.

7.4 Monitoring Performance with Google Analytics and Site Tools

Checking your site's show is head for understanding client leads, following page load speeds, and perceiving regions for streamlining. Instruments like Google Appraisal and other site-checking devices give no-fuss experiences into how guests speak with your site and how immediate satisfaction is conveyed. In this piece, we'll investigate how to set up and utilize Google Appraisal nearby extra site page mechanical congregations to follow and encourage your page's show tenaciously.

Setting Up Google Analytics for Performance Monitoring

Google Evaluation is a free, fundamental asset that tracks guest investments on your site, giving information on assessments like site hits, skip rates, and meeting length, starting there, the sky is the limit. Setting up Google Evaluation starts by making a record at the Google Assessment site, where you'll be facilitated through the most notable way to deal with adding your site as a property and getting an entrancing following ID. This ID is utilized to screen traffic and can be added to WordPress either really in the site's header or through modules like MonsterInsights or Site Pack by Google, which works on the mix cycle.

Exactly when your site is related to finding out about Evaluation, you can give a record of gathering direct, including steady guest information, district, traffic sources, and gadget types. This information helps in understanding client financial aspects, which pages perform best, and where guests will now and again drop off. By perceiving pages with high skip rates or low liability, you can target unequivocal regions for execution updates.

Using Google Analytics Reports to Track Load Times

Notwithstanding guest assessments, Google Assessment offers basic snippets of data into your site's stack times. Under the "Immediate" segment, you can consider the "Site Speed" report, which separates page load times, server reaction times, and other speed assessments. This report gives a wretched gander at how fast each page loads, empowering you to pinpoint slow-stacking pages that could require improvement.

The "Page Timings" subsection inside Site Speed awards you to analyze the heap seasons of individual pages, featuring those that are performing more postponed than run-of-the-mill. Moreover, the "Speed Considerations" report presents express recommendations for extra making inconvenience times, which depend upon Google's PageSpeed Snippets of data. By understanding these contemplations, for example, reducing picture gauges or utilizing program holding, you can allow improvements that will incite quantifiable upgrades in execution.

Implementing Site Monitoring Tools for Real-Time Insights

While Google Evaluation gives sweeping information on client direct and site speed, utilizing committed site checking instruments offers further experiences into uptime, individual time, and other execution assessments. Gadgets like GTmetrix, Pingdom, and UptimeRobot are organized unequivocally for checking site execution, giving unending alarms tolerating your site encounters log sticks or goes withdrew.

These contraptions routinely offer positive reports that incorporate assessments like An Entryway to First Byte (TTFB), load times for individual assets, and recommendations for refreshing each. GTmetrix, for instance, gives a general show score as well as proposes districts for development, for example, compacting JavaScript records or drawing in drowsy stacking. By setting up cautions, you can answer right away on the off chance that your site's show falls under expected rules, limiting edge time and guaranteeing a smooth client experience.

Tracking Core Web Vitals for User Experience Metrics

Google's Center Web Vitals — assessments that action client experience — are principal attributes of site page execution. These vitals unite Most noteworthy Contentful Paint (LCP), which evaluations load time; First Information Deferral (FID), which truly investigates information; and Full-scale Plan Shift (CLS), which surveys visual strength. Meeting these Center Web Vitals rules is legitimately enormous for web search instrument arranging, as Google considers them while closing pursuit positions.

Google Evaluation tracks these assessments fairly, however unambiguous instruments like Google Search Control concentration and Sign arrangement are more serious snippets of data. Google Search Control concentration's "Center Web Vitals" report shows how your page acts when thinking about genuine client information, including regions that need improvement. Signal, open through Chrome's Expert Instruments, drives a show review and gives thoughts to each Center Web Fundamental. Dependably seeing these assessments assists you with guaranteeing your page offers an ideal encounter, further making client fulfillment and Site headway rankings.

Analyzing User Flow and Engagement Metrics

In Google Appraisal, the "Lead Stream" report shows how clients research your site, permitting you to see which pages are the critical segment and leave focuses and how clients progress between them. This report is head for figuring out client obligations and seeing probable bottlenecks. On the off chance that a particular page has a high leave rate, it could show an essential for quicker stacking, an even clearer course, or really convincing substance to keep guests got.

Also, "Objective" going on in Google Evaluation draws you to screen express moves that guests make on your site, like construction sections, buys, or joins up. Portraying up targets can give data into the practicality of show pages and change ways, assisting you with advancing for higher obligation and change rates. With this information, you can make informed acclimations to work on both execution and client experience.

Using Data to Drive Continuous Improvement

With Google Evaluation and site page checking devices set up, dependably examining and returning to execution information is fundamental to keeping areas of strength for a. Month-to-month or quarterly execution surveys award you to recognize plans after some time, showing how changes in satisfied, plan, or advancement influence load rates and client obligation. For instance, following taking care of a CDN, you can see whether influence rates decline on key pages, giving certain affirmations of progress.

By checking these assessments consistently, you can comparably see issues before they arise. Tolerating you notice that heap times are developing throughout a drawn out time, you can investigate late changes —, for example, new modules or more noteworthy media records — that might be influencing execution. Remaining proactive in isolating execution information guarantees that your site stays serious and concurs with best practices.

Building a High-Performing Website with Data-Driven Insights

Checking your page's appearance through Google Evaluation and other site page devices gives a flood of information that is essential for keeping a quick, dependable, and connecting page. By zeroing in on assessments like page load speed, client stream, Center Web Vitals, and obligation, you can go with information-driven choices that dependably further encourage client experience. With standard checking and progress, your WordPress site page can remain receptive to the necessities of your gathering, performing perfectly and accomplishing your site page's objectives.

Chapter 8: SEO and Digital Marketing Strategies for WordPress

Streamlining a WordPress page for web search gadgets and motorized displaying channels is essential to developing its perceivable quality, driving traffic, and accomplishing business targets. Somewhat 8, we'll investigate the key web page upgrade and motorized showing methods of reasoning you want to cultivate your page's web-based presence in 2025. From articulation streamlining and on-page web page smoothing out to content progressing and virtual redirection, these systems will assist with making your WordPress site page solid areas for a resource.

On-Page SEO: Keywords, Titles, and Meta Descriptions

On-page Web improvement starts with key watchword confirmation and situations all through your site. Begin by investigating huge watchwords for your specialty utilizing contraptions like Google Articulation Facilitator, Ahrefs, or SEMrush. Desire to pick both high-volume and long-tail watchwords to expand your potential results arranging across different pursue terms. Place basic articulations in head regions, like the title, meta portrayals, headers, and body message, to improve on happy for web search devices to handle and rank.

Meta depictions and title marks expect a key part in influencing investigate rates from web crawler results pages (SERPs). Making brief and convincing meta portrayals for each page, with articulations conventionally coordinated, further makes search recognizable quality and urges clients to click. Guarantee that all titles, portrayals, and URLs are refreshed for clarity and congruity, as this is an immense process of Google's arranging calculation.

Creating High-Quality Content to Drive Engagement

Content extra parts key to modernized displaying and Web upgrade achievement. Conveying unparalleled grades, and education, and partnering with content that is requested by your gathering maintains your site page's power and positions higher in web crawlers. Blog segments, instructive exercises, coordinates, and mixed media content, similar to accounts and infographics, make your page an immense asset in your specialty. Routinely strengthening substance and adding new, enlightening presents besides flags on web crawlers that your site page is dynamic and current.

Contemplate making foundation or "spot of help" content that covers basic subjects all over, which you can then connect with from related posts on your site. This system updates client experience as well as further makes Web piece overhaul by aiding web records with understanding your page's turn of events and major subjects. For instance, on the off chance that you have a modernized propelling web diary, make expansive partners on center centers like "Website improvement Fundamentals" or "Content Showing Methods" to get your website's point.

Technical SEO: Optimizing Site Speed and Mobile Friendliness

Specific web page improvement integrates moving parts like site page speed, minimized responsiveness, and fitting utilization of HTML marks, which affect search rankings and client experience. Begin by guaranteeing that your site is versatile, as minimal first mentioning has changed into Google's norm. Utilize responsive subjects and test your site's adaptable show on instruments like Google's Dynamic Test.

Site speed is one more fundamental variable, as lethargic stacking pages accomplish high skip rates. Compacting pictures, drawing in lethargic stacking, and utilizing a substance development affiliation (CDN) can essentially furthermore cultivate trouble times. Guarantee that your page structure is great, working with URLs, a sitemap, and clear alt text for pictures, which helps the web with glancing through gadgets slither and record your substance significantly more.

Leveraging Social Media to Amplify Reach

Virtual redirection is a key piece of motorized showing that redesigns your substance and drives traffic back to your site. Stages like Facebook, Twitter, LinkedIn, and Instagram allow you to share your WordPress content with a more noteworthy gathering, assisting work with really taking a look at care and obligation. Coordinate social sharing buttons on blog entries and key pages to urge guests to share your substance on their own profiles.

While coordinating your web-based entertainment approach, spin around making content that is both useful and shareable. Drawing in pictures, titles, and subtitles affects getting thought and developing investigative rates. Tailor your substance to suit each stage's gathering and course of action, and consider utilizing virtual redirection the heap up contraptions like Hootsuite or Sponsorship to plan and track your posts for reliable obligation.

Building Backlinks for Authority and SEO

Backlinks — joins from different objections to your substance — are fundamental workout web crawler assessments, as they show dependability and congruity. Fabricating top-notch backlinks fans out your site as a genuine asset, inducing better rankings. Begin by connecting with suitable objections, online journals, and powerhouses in your specialty to fan out affiliations or visitors posting open entrances that give joins back to your webpage.

Making shareable substance, such as infographics or pro gatherings, can draw in typical backlinks. Outside interface establishment ought to be done charmingly, and keep away from "dull cap" techniques like buying joins, as these can incite disciplines from web records. Considering everything, spin around ordinary external association establishment strategies by giving basic substance that others in your industry will conventionally need to share and reference.

Using Analytics to Measure Success and Refine Strategies

Following the adequacy of your Site progression and modernized showing endeavors is vital for consistent improvement. Use Google Appraisal, Google Search Control Center, and other assessment instruments to screen key assessments like customary traffic, change rates, skip rates, and client leads. Dismantling this information can uncover which approaches are driving the most traffic and changes and component regions that could require change.

Site headway and advancing are iterative cycles, so consistently researching your show and changing your method considering information is critical. Put forward sensible focuses for assessments like site visits, investigate rates, and changes, and use them to quantify your progress. By reliably refining your systems, you can foster a fair, solid modernized showing plan that assists your WordPress with siting flourish.

Building a Sustainable SEO and Digital Marketing Strategy

Overpowering Web piece improvement and motorized displaying on WordPress requires a fair methodology that sets specific streamlining, uncommon substance, and key movement. By zeroing in on client experience, partnering with content, and legitimate backlinks, you can furthermore encourage your advantage rankings and drive more traffic. With the right blend of Site smoothing out methodology and modernized displaying attempts, your WordPress website page can accomplish more prominent perceivable quality, reach, and effect in a constant significant level scene.

8.1 Keyword Research and On-Page SEO

Keyword research and on-page Webpage upgrade structure the supporting of a convincing WordPress page that draws in ordinary active time gridlock and positions well in web crawlers. To execute these methods of reasoning, it's important to comprehend how to see high-respect watchwords and apply them unequivocally inside your substance and site structure.

Understanding Keyword Research: The Foundation of SEO

Articulation research is the most broadly perceived way to deal with perceiving the pursuit terms clients go into web crawlers while searching for content proper to your page's solidarity. This getting ready assists you with understanding the language your gathering utilizes and the particular centers they're amped up for, directing you toward making content that settles their issues. Begin by conceptualizing a synopsis of subjects related to your site and use articulation research instruments like Google Watchword Facilitator, Ahrefs, or SEMrush to uncover related articulations, search volumes, and challenge levels. By exploring both high-volume and specialty long-tail articulations, you can shape a reasonable system that objectives serious and fundamentally unambiguous solicitation terms.

While isolating watchwords, search for terms with basic pursuit volume at any rate generally low dispute, as these can frequently convey the best outcomes. Long-tail articulations — longer verbalizations with lower search volumes at any rate higher unequivocality — are basic for driving alloted traffic to your site. For instance, on the off chance that you run a WordPress blog about motorized propelling, a high-volume watchword may be "Web creation improvement tips," while a more specialty long-tail articulation could be "Webpage improvement tips for WordPress learners."

Implementing Keywords in Key On-Page Elements

Whenever you've picked the right watchwords, convincingly coordinate them into focal on-page parts. Begin by setting the major articulation inside the page's title, as it helps web documents understand the page's center subject. A convincing, articulation-rich title manages your Site improvement as well as hypnotizes clients to click. Guarantee each title is extraordinary and illuminating, unequivocally mirroring the substance on the page.

Meta depictions, the short once-overs that show up under titles being referred to things, ought to correspondingly combine your basic articulation. Despite the way that meta depictions don't impact rankings, they impact investigation rates, which can by idea influence Web improvement execution. Structure brief, partner with meta portrayals that surely frame what perusers can anticipate from the page. Counting watchwords conventionally inside the hidden 100 enunciations of your substance, as well as in the focal headings (H1, H2), assists web search gadgets with figuring out the crucial subjects.

Enhancing Content with Keywords: Placement and Density

Sorting out watchwords really inside your substance body is fundamental, yet balance is key to keep away from articulation stuffing — a planning that can impel disciplines. Bet everything situation, utilizing indistinguishable words and related terms to remain mindful of fathomability and appeal to web records. Utilize the major articulation on various occasions inside the substance, including inside the fundamental region, to hail its congruity to web documents. LSI (Latent Semantic Mentioning) watchwords — related terms and explanations — can in this way be critical, as they assist with looking through motors to handle the setting of your substance.

Subheadings (H2, H3) are huge spaces for right-hand watchwords and add to the client experience by making content all the more clear to research. Segregating long blocks of text with watchword-rich subheadings overhauls clearness as well as awards web records to make sense of the advancement of your substance. Also, consolidating articulations in picture alt texts, subtitles, and record names permits extra chances to web examine contraption mentioning and further makes openness for clearly hindered clients.

Optimizing URL Structure and Internal Links

Your URL structure is one more on-page Web improvement part where articulations can update your website's perceptible quality. Utilize short, mesmerizing URLs that unite gigantic articulations, and take the necessary steps not to utilize complex pictures or numbers, as immaculate URLs are more detectable to the two clients and web crawlers. A URL like "example.com/site improvement tips-for-youths" is more clear and more sensible than "example.com/page?id=1234."

Interior partner, or interacting with different pages inside your site, fans out your site's turn of events and keeps guests related longer. Partnering with significant internal pages involving attracting anchor text containing articulations makes an unparalleled client experience and helps the web with glancing through gadgets in understanding your site page's substance demand. In like manner, it conveys interface regard across your site, managing the arranging limit of additional pages.

Monitoring Keyword Performance with Analytics

At the point when you've done your watchword and on-page Site smoothing out systems, checking their show is fundamental to refining your strategy. Devices like Google Evaluation and Google Search Control Center give experiences into watchword rankings, normal traffic, and investigation rates. Dependably survey which watchwords are driving traffic and which pages are performing great or forgetting to compare suspicions. This information allows you to make changes, for example, strengthening substance with articulations that have shown appropriate or re-streamlining failing to compare suspicions pages.

Separate assessments like bob rates, time on page, and changes to assess how well your demeanor procedure lines up with the client plan. If unambiguous pages draw in guests in any case negligence to keep them pulled in, consider adjusting the substance or watchword strategy to ensure a better match of what clients are looking for. By dependably chipping away at considering execution information, you can change your watchword research and on-page Site improvement strategies to upgrade your WordPress website page's distinguishable quality and significance.

In light of everything, administering articulation research and on-page Site improvement spreads out serious strong regions for a point for motorized propelling achievement. Through crucial watchword position, streamlining on-page parts, and consistent seeing, you could on an extremely essential level further cultivate your site page's web at any point record execution, and gather reach.

8.2 Integrating Google Analytics and Search Console

Planning Google Assessment and Google Search Control focus with your WordPress webpage is critical for understanding how visitors help out your webpage and how it acts in web crawler results. These astonishing resources give critical encounters into your site's traffic, client direct, and Website streamlining execution, helping you with making informed decisions to redesign your webpage's compass and ampleness.

Setting Up Google Analytics on WordPress

Google Examination is a crucial gadget for following and analyzing site traffic. It gives point-by-point data about how clients find and helps out your site, allowing you to evaluate estimations like gatherings, bounce rates, traffic sources, client economics, and change rates. To set up Google Examination on your WordPress site, the underlying step is to make a Google Assessment account if you haven't at this point. At the point when your record is set up, Google will make the following code.

To integrate Google Assessment with WordPress, you can either truly add the accompanying code to your site's header or use a module. The manual method incorporates getting to the "header.php" record in your WordPress subject and implanting the accompanying code before the end </head> tag. For clients who favor a more direct philosophy, there are a couple of modules open, for instance, "MonsterInsights" or "GA Google Examination," that license you to quickly consolidate Google Assessment without hoping to code. At the point when the blend is done, you can start gathering data about your site's show.

Understanding Key Metrics in Google Analytics

At the point when Google Assessment is set up, understanding key estimations and reports is essential for seeking data-driven decisions. Unquestionably the main estimations include:

- **Sessions and Users**: This shows the number of people that have visited your site, with gatherings tending to individual visits and clients exhibiting the number of outstanding visitors.
- **Traffic Sources**: This report nuances where your website traffic comes from, including normal chase, paid search, online diversion, direct visits, and references.
- **Bounce Rate**: The sway rate exhibits the degree of visitors who leave your site to survey just a single page. A high skip rate can

mean that your substance isn't interfacing with or relevant to the clients.

- **Average Session Duration**: This estimation tells you how long clients stay on your site in general. Longer gatherings oftentimes exhibit better client responsibility and significant substance.
- **Goal Conversions**: Google Assessment grants you to advance up targets, (for instance, structure passages or thing purchases), helping you with following the sufficiency of your site in achieving business objectives.

By reliably examining these estimations, you can recognize districts for advancement, for instance, high skip rates or low responsibility, and take action to work on your site's show.

Setting Up Google Search Console

Google Search Control focus is one more valuable resource that helps you with noticing your webpage's Internet improvement execution and detectable quality in Google Question things. Not the slightest bit like Google Examination, which focuses on client leads on your page, Search Control focus gives pieces of information into how Google views and downers your site. To set up Google Search Control focus, you need to add and look at your site in the gadget. This ought to be conceivable through a couple of techniques, for instance, adding an HTML record to your site or checking ownership through your space selection focus.

At the point when your page is checked, Google Search Control focus will start gathering data about your site's request execution. You'll have the choice to see which search questions convey traffic to your site, the number of impressions (how much of the time your site appears in list things), and the dynamic clicking factor (CTR) for your pages. You can moreover see the regular spot of your pages in question things, helping you with following how well your substance positions for assigned watchwords.

Leveraging Search Console's SEO Insights

Google Search Control focus gives principal Web streamlining encounters that can help with fostering your website's web list rankings. Unquestionably the main reports in Search Control focus include:

- **Performance Report**: This shows quick and dirty data about how your pages act in Google search, including clicks, impressions, typical position, and CTR for each inquiry. Taking apart this report helps you understand which expressions are guiding individuals to your site and where there may be possible opportunities to improve for better rankings.
- **Index Coverage Report**: This report shows how well your pages are requested by Google. It separates any crawl missteps or pages that are not being recorded, allowing you to fix gives that could unfavorably influence your web search instrument detectable quality.
- **Sitemaps**: You can introduce your sitemap to investigate through Search Control focus, ensuring that all of your pages are recorded fittingly. Regularly taking a gander at the circumstance with your sitemap ensures that Google can find and crawl limitlessly huge pages on your site.
- **Mobile Usability Report**: Google Search Control focus moreover gives encounters into how well your site performs on PDAs. Since convenient first requesting is right now indispensable for Google,

keeping an eye on any flexible convenience issues is basic for Site advancement accomplishment.

Integrating Google Analytics and Search Console for Holistic Insights

While both Google Examination and Google Search Control focus give significant encounters freely, integrating them can furnish you with a more careful point of view on your site's show. By associating your Google Examination account with Google Search Control focus, you can get to glance through question data clearly inside your Assessment dashboard. This mix licenses you to see which normal pursuit requests convey visitors to your site and how those clients team up with your substance.

In Google Assessment, you can see reports that combine both the social data from the Assessment and the chase execution data from the Search Control focus. This blend enables you to seek after data-driven decisions, for instance, overhauling neglecting to measure up to assumptions pages or dealing with fulfilled-to-target high-traffic watchwords. It furthermore allows you to measure how well your Web architecture upgrade attempts convert into critical exercises, similar to changes or arrangements.

Planning Google Examination and Google Search Control focus with your WordPress site is a major stage toward getting a handle on your site's presentation and dealing with its detectable quality. These instruments give huge pieces of information into client direct, traffic sources, and Web architecture upgrade execution, helping you with recognizing open entryways for smoothing out. By reliably inspecting the data from the two phases, you can seek informed decisions that lead to more promptly web crawler rankings, extended traffic, and a seriously convincing website.

8.3 Social Media and Content Marketing Tactics

In the current significant level world, sorting out electronic entertainment with your substance displaying philosophy is essential for building brand care, directing people to your WordPress site page, and drawing in with your gathering. Virtual redirection stages offer a sharp procedure for arriving at a colossal gathering, while content hoisting licenses you to offer some benefit, show mastery, and place of collaboration with expected clients. Solid web-based entertainment and content-showing frameworks can assist you with cultivating your electronic presence and fostering significant length relationships with your gathering.

Understanding the Role of Social Media in Content Marketing

Online redirection is a significant asset for flowing substance, drawing in with partners, and making discussions around your image. By sharing site segments, accounts, infographics, and different sorts of content on stages like Facebook, Twitter, Instagram, LinkedIn, and TikTok, you can contact a more prominent gathering of past individuals who visit your website page straightforwardly. Virtual entertainment expands your substance's compass, broadening distinguishable quality and driving traffic back to your site.

Persuading substance showing, then again, is associated with making basic and pertinent substance uncommonly intended to your vested party's inclinations, necessities, and trouble spots. Right when you coordinate electronic redirection with your substance-propelling endeavors, you can make a remarkable data circle where your gathering helps shape your substance technique, and your substance drives social obligation.

Creating Engaging Social Media Content

To really incorporate virtual redirection for content propelling, your substance should draw in and be expected for each stage's excellent plan. Each virtual redirection stage has its own style and gathering speculations, so the substance you present ought to on be changed as required.

For instance, on stages like Instagram and Pinterest, visual substance, for example, five-star pictures and records perform best. A blog section shared on these stages ought to have an eye-getting picture and a convincing subtitle to stand out. On Twitter, short, splendid messages with important hashtags and a relationship with your substance are solid. LinkedIn, with its more expert multitude, is more prepared for complete articles, setting focused examinations, and industry experiences.

As well as sharing site areas, accounts, and infographics, you ought to in this way ponder making content that maintains joint effort, like audits, tests, and questions. Drawing in with your gathering through electronic redirection remarks and direct messages assists in fabricating an area of your substance, which with canning further cultivates brand responsibility and desire with reiterating visits to your site.

Repurposing Content for Maximum Reach

One of the most extraordinary ecstatic propelling techniques is reusing content. By turning blog segments, mechanized imparts, online classes, or records into various plans, you can collect the extent of your substance without making totally new material with no preparation.

For instance, a well-performing blog segment can be changed into an infographic for Pinterest, a development of tweets for Twitter, or a succinct video for Instagram or TikTok. Reusing content awards you to take advantage of various gathering portions on different stages, widening the degree of your unique substance.

Besides, utilizing reused content across electronic redirection stages makes a reliable brand message and supports key subjects, guaranteeing your gathering has different touchpoints with your substance. This system upholds your substance's worth as well as saves time and assets by reusing the work you've as of late situated into making top-notch fulfilled.

Leveraging Influencer Marketing for Expanded Reach

Robust publicizing is one more astounding framework for content spread. By teaming up with rockin' rollers in your industry or strength, you can take advantage of their spread-out gathering and gain responsiveness to new devotees. Rockin' rollers can assist with working on your substance by giving it to their partners, making client-made content, or embracing your things or associations.

While working with powerhouses, it's central to get people whose values line with your image and whose gathering covers your objective segment. By fanning out acceptable relationships with rockin' rollers, you can build more trust with their partners, making it almost certain that they'll to drawn in with your substance and visit your site.

Measuring the Impact of Social Media and Content Marketing

To audit the reasonableness of your electronic entertainment and content-advancing techniques, you should dependably assess key execution pointers (KPIs). Conventional KPIs for online entertainment coordinate liability rates (likes, remarks, shares), partner headway and website page traffic made from virtual redirection channels. For content publicizing, rotate around assessments, for example, time spent on a page, skip rate, change rate, and how intermittently your substance is shared or connected with from different sources.

Instruments like Google Appraisal, online entertainment assessment (like Facebook Experiences or Twitter Evaluation), and unapproachable stages like Hootsuite or Foster Social can assist you with following these KPIs. By taking a gander at these assessments, you can get huge experiences into what kinds of content perform best, which electronic redirection stages are driving the most traffic, and which frameworks are best in accomplishing your advancing objectives.

Optimizing Content for Social Sharing

To manufacture the possible results that your substance will be shared through virtual entertainment, chipping away at your site's substance for social sharing is fundamental. This integrates guaranteeing that your blog areas and different sorts of content have electronic entertainment-sharing buttons effectively available on each page. These buttons award clients to give your substance to their supporters, widening your reach rapidly.

Moreover, you ought to ensure that your substance is enthralling and shareable. This could integrate making eye-getting pictures or pieces that are streamlined for virtual entertainment points of view and plans. Instruments like Canva or Adobe Flash can assist you with making proficient-looking visuals that empower social sharing.

Coordinating electronic redirection and content-propelling techniques is tremendous for cultivating your online presence and expanding your site's traffic. By figuring out the gig of virtual redirection in satisfied development, making drawing in and shareable substance, reusing existing substance, utilizing sensational peculiarity showing, and evaluating your endeavors, you can successfully push your WordPress site and contact a more noteworthy, more pulled-in swarm. Constantly pushing your substance for social sharing and transforming it for various stages will keep your substance new and critical, permitting you to gather more grounded relationships with your gathering and drive extended-length achievement.

8.4 Advanced Strategies: Schema Markup, Featured Snippets, and Core Web Vitals

As web page plan improvement (Web streamlining) grows, undeniable level techniques have emerged to help locales with hanging out in web search apparatus results and further foster detectable quality. While standard Web composition upgrade techniques, for instance, expression improvement and content creation stay major, significant level strategies like planning markup, included pieces, and Center Web Vitals offer additional opportunities to update a web page's Internet streamlining execution. Executing these frameworks can help your WordPress with siting achieve higher rankings, increase explore rates, and further foster client experience, provoking better overall results in web search devices like Google.

Understanding Schema Markup

Synthesis markup is a kind of coordinated data that helps web crawlers get a handle on the setting of your substance. By adding unequivocal HTML names to your website, creation markup enables web crawlers to perceive key information like things, studies, events, articles, and recipes, and that is only the start. This coordinated data is then used through web files to show rich pieces, which are further developed inquiry things that stand separated from ordinary results by showing additional information like evaluations, expenses, and dates.

Executing outline markup on your WordPress webpage can help with fostering your web search apparatus's detectable quality and work on the likelihood of your pages appearing in rich pieces. To add frame markup, you can use modules like Creation Pro or Yoast Site enhancement, which make it more direct to execute coordinated data on your page without requiring wide coding data.

Kinds of example markup that is particularly helpful for WordPress destinations integrate Thing planning, Article charts, Overview arrangement, FAQ diagrams, and How-to frame. By including the appropriate markup for the substance on your webpage, you give web records point-by-point information that can help them with showing more huge and valuable rundown things, finally supporting your rankings and exploring rates.

Featured Snippets: What They Are and How to Optimize for Them

Included pieces are uncommon blocks of information that appear at the most noteworthy mark of Google Question things, regularly suggested as "position zero." These pieces hope to give quick, clear answers to glance through requests without anticipating that clients should tap on an association. Featured pieces can consolidate definitions, records, tables, or steps, and they give an entryway to your site to procure stand-apart property in question things.

To upgrade for featured pieces, it's crucial to make content that answers ordinary requests in your industry. This consolidates using clear, minimized language and coordinating your substance in a way that is straightforward for Google to isolate. For example, using list things for records, numbered adventures for bearings, or clearly described headings for explanations can grow the conceivable outcomes of your substance being picked as an included piece.

You should similarly target long-tail watchwords and question-based search requests, as these will undoubtedly set off included pieces. Instruments like Reaction Everyone or SEMrush can help with recognizing such requests your group is presenting, allowing you to further develop your substance fittingly.

While featured pieces are not guaranteed, updating your substance in this way chips away at the likelihood of being featured. Recall that staying aware of unrivaled grade, genuine substance is essential for staying in featured pieces once your substance is picked.

Core Web Vitals: Measuring and Improving User Experience

Focus Web Vitals are a lot of execution estimations familiar to Google to measure the client experience of a website. These estimations are based on the stacking rate, knowledge, and visual steadfastness of a page. Google includes these signs as situating factors, suggesting that regions with better Center Web Vitals scores will undoubtedly rank higher in question things.

The three key Community Web Vitals estimations are:

- **Largest Contentful Paint (LCP)**: This activity how quickly the greatest recognizable substance part, similar to an image or text, appears on the screen. A speedy LCP ensures that your site stacks quickly, which is central for holding visitors.
- **First Input Delay (FID)**: FID gauges how quickly the site answers a client's most significant collaboration, for instance, clicking a button or investigating an association. A low FID shows that the site is responsive and gives a predominant client experience.
- **Cumulative Layout Shift (CLS)**: CLS gauges the visual steadfastness of a page. A low CLS suggests that parts on the page, such as secures or pictures, don't all of a sudden move around as the page loads, giving a smoother examining experience.

To additionally foster Center Web Vitals on your WordPress site, it's central for base on upgrading your website's speed, responsiveness, and visual strength. This can be achieved by overhauling pictures, using saving and content movement associations (CDNs), restricting JavaScript and CSS records, and utilizing current web developments like detached stacking and strange stacking.

You can screen your website's Middle Web Vitals using gadgets like Google PageSpeed Encounters, which gives pieces of information about how your website page is performing and unequivocal ideas for advancement. Reliably testing your site's Middle Web Vitals ensures that you're giving a speedy and smooth client experience, which is basic for Site improvement in 2025.

Integrating These Strategies for Maximum Impact

To get the full benefit of these general methods, organizing them into your overall Web composition improvement methodology is huge. Design markup, featured pieces, and Center Web Vitals all work together to update the client experience and work on your detectable quality in web crawler results.

Start by adding planning markup to your most critical pages, ensuring that your substance is especially coordinated and can be actually unraveled by means of web search apparatuses. Upgrade for featured pieces by focusing on the most broadly perceived questions your vested party is asking and planning your substance for basic extraction. Finally, center on additional creating Center Web Vitals to overhaul your page's presentation and meet Google's situating rules.

By using these general strategies, you can arrange your WordPress webpage for progress in 2025, driving more traffic, further creating client responsibility, and further developing your web crawler rankings. As Google continues to foster its computations, staying before these examples will ensure your site stays serious in the consistently changing high-level scene.

Chapter 9: Accessibility and Compliance for WordPress Sites

In the present high-level scene, it's a higher need than at some other opportunity to ensure that your WordPress site is available to all clients, regardless of their abilities. Receptiveness suggests the demonstration of making your site usable by people with ineptitudes, and it's a fundamental part of moral reasons as well concerning legal consistency. Likewise, various countries have guidelines and rules that anticipate that locales should be accessible. This part explores how to make an open WordPress site, focusing on the key receptiveness rules, gadgets, and frameworks to help you adjust to accessibility standards and assurance that your substance contacts a greater group.

Why Accessibility Matters for WordPress Websites

Site transparency is central to inclusivity. A site that is open can be used by people with various impairments, such as visual prevention, hearing hardship, motor ineptitudes, and mental incapacities. According to the World Prosperity Affiliation, more than 1 billion people generally live with an impediment, and that suggests that arranging locales considering receptiveness can on a very basic level broaden your group.

From a real position, forgetting to fulfill transparency rules could open your site to claims. In various districts, for instance, the US and European Affiliation, receptiveness is directed by guidelines like the Americans with Impediment Act (ADA) and the European Web Accessibility Order. These rules anticipate that locales should give a comparable experience to people with impediments, and failure to assent could achieve fines or genuine outcomes.

Also, an accessible site further creates convenience for all clients, notwithstanding those with handicaps. Huge quantities of the systems used to further develop transparency — like clear course, explaining alt text, and authentic contrast — also redesign client experience for all visitors. As web crawlers continuously center on client experience, accessibility redesigns can moreover help your Site improvement execution.

Understanding Accessibility Standards and Guidelines

To ensure that your webpage satisfies transparency rules, it's indispensable to have a lot of familiarity with the Web Content Accessibility Rules (WCAG), which are a lot of worldwide principles made by the Web Consortium (W3C). WCAG outlines four essential norms of accessibility:

- **Perceivable**: Content ought to be presented in habits that clients can see, including offering message decisions for non-message content and making media accessible for all clients.
- **Operable**: Clients ought to have the choice to investigate and connect with content, including offering console receptiveness and offering adequate chances to clients to examine and team up with content.
- **Understandable**: Information and the UI ought to be clear and direct, with an obvious approach to acting and understandable text.
- **Robust**: Content ought to be reasonable with current and future advances, ensuring that assistive developments can get to and interpret content.

WCAG gives unequivocal models to these guidelines at different levels of conformance (A, AA, and AAA). Most locales hope to meet the AA level, which integrates huge guidelines for transparency that will cover the majority of clients with inadequacies.

WordPress Accessibility Features and Tools

WordPress is centered on making site design open and offers a couple of basic features and instruments to help siting owners satisfy transparency rules. Normally, WordPress subjects and modules are expected to agree to WCAG rules, but it's basic to affirm that your point and modules remain totally accessible.

Various WordPress subjects are transparently arranged, and that suggests they follow the acknowledged systems for accessible site engineering. These subjects integrate features like clear course, text-based content for screen perusers, and sponsorship for console courses. Anyway, not all subjects are made the same, and some could require additional customization to totally observe receptiveness rules.

There are a couple of gadgets available for testing and further creating receptiveness in WordPress regions. Modules like WP Transparency, Accessibility Checker, and A solitary Tick Accessibility give basic strategies for completing components, for instance, text style resizing, skip course associations, and separation overhauls. These modules can help ensure that your site adjusts to key transparency rules, making it more direct for clients with ineptitudes to investigate your substance.

For additional created accessibility testing, you can use untouchable mechanical assemblies like WAVE (Web Receptiveness Appraisal Instrument), Reference point, and Ax to channel your page for accessibility issues. These devices will highlight the district of your site that needs improvement, for instance, missing alt text, unseemly heading development, or assortment contrast issues.

Ensuring Accessibility for Media and Content

Pictures, accounts, and other blended media parts are a significant part of the time dismissed concerning accessibility, yet they can be essential for ensuring a thorough experience. For pictures, you should constantly consolidate alt text, a short portrayal of the image's substance, which licenses screen perusers to give the image to blocked clients. The alt text should depict the substance or ability of the image with the end goal that building the worth of the client's understanding, rather than essentially portraying it.

For video content, giving captions and records is basic for clients who are deaf or almost hard of hearing. WordPress maintains the embedding of video content from stages like YouTube and Vimeo, which bargain robotized writing, but it's not startling critical to actually review and change these engravings for precision. Additionally, offering sound portrayals for visual substance, especially in instructive accounts, can help those with visual impedances better handle the substance.

While embedding media, ensure that each instinctive part — like affixes or controls inside accounts — is accessible through the control center and screen perusers. Guaranteeing that blended media content is properly marked and open contributes out and out to meeting WCAG leads and overhauling client experience.

Legal Compliance and Accessibility Audits

Consistency with transparency guidelines is a pivotal idea for WordPress site owners, particularly in locales with extreme rules. As well as complying with WCAG rules, associations ought to moreover sort out their local guidelines. For example, in the US, the ADA expects that public locales be available to individuals with handicaps. Failure to observe these rules could incite legal movement.

Standard accessibility audits are major to ensure nonstop consistency. These surveys should review both the substance and convenience of the site, perceiving and changing any issues that could obstruct access for clients with handicaps. Performing surveys reliably — especially after critical updates or design changes — ensure that your site stays accessible and pleasant with creating rules.

WordPress offers various modules and outcast organizations that can assist with receptiveness audits. Coordinating these really looks to intentionally decline genuine risks as well as further foster your site's overall client experience.

Making an accessible WordPress site is fundamental for developing your group and ensuring that everyone, paying little notice to limit, can investigate and team up with your site. By complying with WCAG rules, using WordPress' accessibility features, and driving standard surveys, you can make an exhaustive, legitimately reliable site. Embracing transparency helps you with reaching a greater group as well as positions your site as one that spotlights convenience, value, and ethical constraints.

9.1 Understanding Accessibility Standards (WCAG 2.1)

Site openness is indispensable for guarantee that everybody, incorporating individuals with handicaps, can get to and collaborate with your site. The Internet Content Straightforwardness Rules (WCAG) 2.1 are a ton of overall rules made by the Internet Consortium (W3C) to make web content more open. These standards are a urgent asset for web subject matter experts and content fashioners, and understanding them can assist with guaranteeing that your WordPress page is usable by individuals with different deficiencies, including visual, hear-able, engine, and mental shortcomings. This part dives into the significance of WCAG 2.1, what it incorporates, and how it very well may be applied to your site.

What is WCAG 2.1?

The Internet Content Openness Rules (WCAG) 2.1 foster WCAG 2.0, which was conveyed in 2008. The standards give clear guidelines on the most proficient procedure to make web content more open to individuals, not permanently set up to encourage availability across various gadgets and progressions furthermore. WCAG 2.1, conveyed in June 2018, encourages the 2.0 principles by including extra recommendation that address the necessities of individuals with mental and learning handicaps, as well as clients on cells.

WCAG 2.1 is created into four critical standards: Indisputable, Operable, Reasonable, and Solid. These rules guarantee that web content is accessible to all clients, paying little heed to what their capacities or the contraptions they use.

The Four Principles of WCAG 2.1

- **Perceivable**: The truly standard splendid lights on ensuring that data on your site is introduced in propensities that clients can see. This incorporates giving text decisions to non-text content, making media content like records available through subtitles, and guaranteeing acceptable partition among text and foundation tones. The objective is to guarantee that all clients, combining those with visual and hear-proficient idiocies, can see your site's substance through various material channels.
- **Operable**: This standard guarantees that clients can research and associate with all merry on the site. This coordinates giving control community openness to clients who can't utilize a mouse and guaranteeing that every single insightful part, as gets and interfaces, are available. It in this way consolidates guaranteeing that clients have satisfactory opportunity to examine and speak with content and giving make course ways to deal with essential authorization to various locale of the site.
- **Understandable**: The substance and the plan of the site ought to be immediate and self-evident. This merges guaranteeing that text is clear and direct, and that the worth of the site acts in a normal way. For instance, designs ought to give clear guidelines, bungle messages ought to be clear, and language ought to be key and direct. This standard is particularly basic for clients with mental disappointments, likewise concerning individuals who could experience issues making sense of perplexing language or course.
- **Robust**: The last rule features the significance of building objections that capacity exceptionally with current and future movements. A decent page ought to be sensible with assistive headways, like screen perusers or voice confirmation programming, and ought to stay utilitarian as web pushes make.

Guaranteeing that your site is sensible with a huge number of contraptions and tasks is essential to making it open to all clients.

Levels of Conformance: A, AA, and AAA

WCAG 2.1 shows three degrees of conformance: A, AA, and AAA. These levels display the truth of openness issues and the necessity for watching out for them.

- **Level A**: This is the base degree of conformance. Locale that dismissal to meet Level A standards will have huge cutoff points for clients with deficiencies. These issues ought to be would overall right away, as they are all around significant for major openness.
- **Level AA**: This is the degree of conformance that most regions ought to endeavor to meet. Level AA coordinates more noteworthy rules that address the essentials of clients with hindrances, and districts that satisfy these guidelines will give a tremendously better encounter than all clients. Most responsiveness reviews and consistence necessities spin around Level AA conformance.
- **Level AAA**: This level watches out for the most developed responsiveness needs and gives the most raised level of conformance. While it is ideal to have a go at AAA conformance, it may not generally be doable for each site, reliant upon its substance and reason. Anyway, looking out for anything that number AAA measures as would be wise will chip away at the openness of your site for clients with unequivocal necessities.

WCAG 2.1 Guidelines in Practice

To apply WCAG 2.1 norms to your WordPress site, there are several phases you can take. Begin by picking an availability organized topic, as these subjects are organized thinking about openness, including appropriate heading structures, contrast degrees, and control focus course. Then, at that point, use modules and contraptions to check your site's openness consistence and fix any issues, for example, missing alt text for pictures, horrifying arrangement contrast, or far away designs.

Standard availability reviews, utilizing instruments like Sign, Hatchet, or WAVE, can help you perceive and address any responsiveness obstructions. Also, while making content, follow best practices for making it open by utilizing reasonable heading names, giving attracting affiliations, and guaranteeing mixed media content is available through inscriptions or records.

By sticking to WCAG 2.1, you can make a greater and easy to use site that is accessible to all guests, paying little heed to what their capacities. These guidelines assist you with staying away from expected genuine difficulties as well as confirmation that your site contacts a more prominent gathering and gives a fair online comprehension to everybody.

Understanding WCAG 2.1 is essential for any website specialist or page proprietor who is based on making their website page open. By seeing the standards displayed in WCAG 2.1, you can guarantee that your WordPress site gives a preferable encounter over clients with obstruction and consents to responsiveness rules. The objective isn't just to meet legitimate prerequisites yet despite make a more complete, clear site that offers worth to a substitute degree of guests.

9.2 Making Your Website ADA Compliant

Ensuring that your WordPress webpage is reliable with the Americans with Insufficiencies Act (ADA) is an urgent piece of building a complete and open electronic presence. The ADA, a social freedoms guideline in the US, orders that all individuals, consolidating those with handicaps, have comparable permission to public organizations and offices. This integrates destinations, which are seen as spots of public comfort under the ADA. Causing your site ADA reliable not simply helps you with avoiding conceivable genuine risks yet moreover ensures that you are offering a site that is available to everyone. This section explores the key advances related with making your WordPress site ADA pleasant and open to clients with various impediment.

Understanding ADA Website Compliance

The ADA doesn't have express concentrated requirements for destinations, but it expects that associations ensure that their web based stages are accessible to people with inadequacies. The law references the standards set by WCAG (Web Content Receptiveness Rules) as a benchmark for website accessibility. While the real ADA doesn't explicitly arrange consistency with WCAG, courts, and regulatory bodies oftentimes suggest these principles while reviewing transparency. For a site to be ADA-reliable, it ought to be usable by individuals with different failures, consolidating those with visual, hear-capable, motor, and mental handicaps.

The ADA doesn't describe a specific breaking point for consistency, so the general supposition that will be that a site should give identical permission to all clients, regardless of what their abilities or inadequacies. This can be achieved by keeping the guidelines of transparency outlined in WCAG 2.1, ensuring that content is recognizable, operable, sensible, and solid.

Key Areas for ADA Compliance

1. Text Alternatives for Non-Text Content

One of the fundamental receptiveness essentials is to give message choices (alt message) for non-message content, similar to pictures, accounts, and plans. Alt text helps clients who with relying upon screen perusers or other assistive advances to get a handle on the substance and justification behind visual parts. Each image or non-text part on your site should have a drawing in and brief alt text that unequivocally reflects its significance or ability. For accounts and sound substance, giving engravings and records is essential for clients with hearing deterrents.

2. Accessible Navigation and Structure

Ensuring your site's course is natural and accessible is another vital area of ADA consistency. All clients, integrating those with inadequacies, ought to have the choice to effectively investigate your site. This consolidates ensuring that your site's menu structure is clear and honestly organized. The usage of open course features, similar to comfort course, is huge for clients with motor obstructions who will not be able to use a mouse. Additionally, the site's organization should be planned to work outstandingly with assistive advances like screen perusers, which read the substance resoundingly.

3. Color Contrast and Visual Elements

Assortment contrast is significant for making content understood, particularly for clients with visual impedances like fractional visual deficiency. To meet ADA necessities, ensure that there is sufficient contrast among text and establishment tones. This is particularly critical for body text, headings, and associations. Do whatever it takes not to include assortment as the principal technique for passing on critical information, as specific clients will in all likelihood not be able to perceive explicit tones. High-contrast assortment designs further foster clarity for clients with low vision and help ensure that your site content is available to all visitors.

4. Accessible Forms

Structures are an essential piece of various destinations, especially for online business regions or objections that require client association. To make your designs ADA-pleasant, ensure that they are suitably checked and coordinated. Each field in construction should have an unquestionable and illustrative name, and good messages should be valuable and clear. For clients relying upon screen perusers, it is important that the construction parts are suitably marked with HTML for similitude. Additionally, giving satisfactory rules and offering elective procedures for submitting information can ensure that all clients can complete designs on your site.

5. Keyboard Accessibility

A significant piece of ADA consistency is ensuring that all site capacities are open through a control center. Various clients with motor shortcomings rely upon a console course as opposed to a mouse. It is basic to guarantee that clients can get to all district of your site and perform significant exercises, (for instance, introducing a design, investigating through joins, or helping out menus) using simply a control center. This consolidates ensuring that tab orders are genuine, focus markers are recognizable, and shrewd parts are quite easy to get to using console substitute ways.

Tools and Plugins to Help Achieve ADA Compliance

There are a couple of WordPress modules and instruments open that can help you ensure ADA consistency on your site. These gadgets can audit your site for accessibility issues, give thoughts for updates, and give continuous fixes to typical transparency issues.

Accessibility Plugins

A couple of modules can help you with making your site ADA-steady by watching out for various transparency needs. Modules, for instance, WP Accessibility and A solitary Tick Receptiveness add features like open course, leap to-content associations, and control center course. Besides, these modules can help with adding alt text for pictures, further foster construction receptiveness, and change contrast extents.

Accessibility Testing Tools

To study the accessibility of your site and check for any encroachment of ADA standards, you can use robotized testing gadgets like WAVE, Ax, and Guide. These gadgets examine your site and produce a record of districts that need improvement, such as missing alt text, insufficient contrast, or challenges to arrive at a course. Standard surveys using these instruments will help with ensuring your site stays steady as you add new blissful or make revives.

Continuous Monitoring and Updating

ADA consistency is a nonstop cycle. As web headways create and new blissful is added to your page, it's indispensable to regularly study and update your webpage's transparency features. This can consolidate testing new themes or modules, ensuring that new blissful is open, and getting back to your site's course and development for continued with accommodation.

Likewise, remembering clients with handicaps for the testing framework can give significant analysis and help you with making imperative acclimations to your site's receptiveness features.

Making your WordPress site ADA-predictable isn't just about social event legal necessities — it's connected to ensuring comparable access and giving a positive client experience to all visitors. By focusing in on receptiveness norms like text decisions, accessible course, and assortment contrast, and by using gadgets to screen and work on your page's consistency, you can make a site that is welcoming to everyone. ADA consistency could require some work, yet the result is a site that is complete, open, and better arranged to serve an alternate extent of clients.

9.3 Tips for Inclusive Design and Usability

Making an expansive site goes past guaranteeing straightforwardness; it is associated with building an encounter that everybody, paying little mind to what their capacities are, can interact with. Complete plan based on convenience, fair access, and savvy client encounters for a wide degree of people, coordinating those with disappointments. By combining comprehensive plan standards, you can make a site that arrangements with different necessities while likewise overhauling in general comfort. This part offers fundamental approaches to making your WordPress site more comprehensive and usable.

Focus on Clear and Simple Navigation

The course is a support of solace. A trademark course structure guarantees that all clients, paying little heed to their experience or cutoff points, can find what they need with inconsequential exertion. For people with mental hindrances or individuals who are new to your site, ease is essential. A prompt menu plan, with plainly named segments, diminishes mental weight and guides clients to their protests significantly more usefully.

For instance, think about disconnecting your course into brief classes, for example, "About," "Associations," "Blog," and "Contact," as opposed to over-upsetting the menu with such endless choices. Plus, consider doing an unrefined or fixed course bar, which licenses clients to get to the menu from any piece of the page without recalling the top.

Prioritize Readability and Legibility

The game plan of text on your site could from an overall perspective at any point impact how clients draw in with your substance. A perfect, noticeable text style is vital for clients with visual impedances, like low vision or deficient visual hindrances. Select text-based styles that are not difficult to analyze, such as sans-serif choices, and try not to preposterously inhale new live into text styles that can be trying to loosen up. Guarantee your text angles are sufficiently gigantic to be reasonable, particularly for body text and headings, and take the necessary steps not to utilize insignificant text-based styles that could cause strain.

Variety contrast is another crucial part. The text should stand isolated obviously against the foundation to oblige clients with visual inadequacies or mostly visual lack. Instruments like the WebAIM Variety Division Checker can assist you with ensuring that your grouping plot observes availability guidelines. By offering high partition among text and foundation, you assist with guaranteeing clarity for all clients.

Design with Flexible and Responsive Layouts

A responsive game plan is fundamental in making your site usable across different contraptions and screen sizes. With additional individuals getting the opportunity to districts on cells, it's vital to make plans that change each chance to various screen widths. A responsive WordPress subject will change content setup typically, guaranteeing that clients can without a truly momentous stretch research your site whether they are utilizing a cell phone, tablet, or PC.

It is moreover principal to consider how content is introduced on little screens. Smaller clients could battle to interact with amassed or complex plans. Go for the stars, moderate plan on versatile perspectives, with contact overall around organized buttons and monster astute regions to encourage ease of use.

Use Alt Text and Descriptive Labels

For clients depending upon screen perusers, alt message (elective message) anticipates a principal part in making heads or tails of visual substance. While adding pictures, guarantee you unite enlightening alt message that addresses the picture's ability or importance. Keep away from sketchy depictions like "picture" or "photograph" and all things considered give the setting, for example, "A lady with little hair sitting at a work area dealing with a PC."

Notwithstanding pictures, give clear, limited marks for each and every sagacious part, for example, buttons, structure fields, and affiliations. An illustrative name tells clients the defense behind the button or the data expected in a plan field. For instance, rather than utilizing nonexclusive text like "Submit," use "Seek after Our Notification" to give clients an even clearer awareness of what activity they are performing.

Create Consistent and Predictable Interactions

A site that routinely assists clients with feeling even more specific when researching it. Consistency across pages works for clients to figure out a good method for interfacing with your site and finding what they need rapidly. For example, buttons ought to have strong plans and conditions across the site, and shrewd parts ought to be not difficult to see.

Moreover, consider how affiliations act. Clients with engine debilitations could depend upon consoles or assistive contraptions of course, so it's fundamental to guarantee that all affiliations are reachable through the control community and that affiliations open in a tantamount window to the side still hanging out there in any case.

Incorporate User Feedback and Testing

No game plan is awesome, particularly concerning inclusivity and comfort. Gathering input obviously from clients is one of the most bewildering ways to deal with guaranteeing that your site is watching out for their necessities. Contact clients with different foundations, unite those with idiocies, and sell their examination on the ease of use of your site.

Client testing can uncover potential issues that you probably won't have noticed. For instance, somebody with dyslexia could find express text testing to examine considering its text-based style or dividing. By drawing in with authentic clients, you can decide these issues before they influence the more prominent gathering.

Despite speedy client input, exploit instruments that duplicate different availability needs. Instruments like WAVE or Hatchet award you to test your site's availability and perceive districts for progression, from console course issues to missing alt text.

Avoid Overloading Users with Information

Mental over-inconvenience is a hindrance for specific clients, particularly those with thought lacks or learning disappointments. Keep your substance fundamental, brief, and compelling. Use headings and subheadings to separate colossal blocks of text, and give clear requests to take action.

On structures, for instance, basically request the huge data, and use multi-step structures whenever required. This approach can keep clients away from feeling overpowered by a preposterous number of fields in one go.

An intensive plan is associated with making a site experience that is inviting and open to all clients, paying little mind to their capacities. By zeroing in on a clear course, reasonable text-based styles, flexible plans, enlightening names, and client examination, you guarantee that your site is usable and drawing in for a more noteworthy gathering. Straightforwardness isn't just about friendly event-certified necessities — it's associated with making a positive client experience that engages everybody to collaborate with no issue by any stretch of the imagination. Embracing total course of action rules makes your site more usable, productive, and open to all, guaranteeing that everybody has tantamount consent to the substance and associations you offer.

9.4 Tools for Testing and Improving Accessibility

Automated Accessibility Testing Tools

Mechanized straightforwardness testing contraptions can rapidly investigate your site and perceive conventional openness issues, giving strong regions for an extra client experience. WAVE (Web Straightforwardness Assessment Contraption) is one of the most outstanding motorized testing instruments, offering a program improvement that sees bungles like missing alt text, ill-advised headings, and low collection contrast. Hatchet, another fundamental asset, sorts out straightforwardly into Chrome and Firefox's fashioner instruments, permitting you to check a page's consistency with Web Content Openness Rules (WCAG) rules during the improvement cycle. Mechanized gadgets alone can't get each openness issue, however, they can for the most part diminish commonplace fumbles without even batting an eye.

Manual Testing for In-Depth Analysis

While mechanized contraptions give a decent beginning stage, manual testing ponders a more expansive assessment. One manual strategy is console essentially course testing, reflecting how clients with engine impairments could associate with your site. Utilizing essentially the "Tab" key, you can test if every regular part — like gets, plans, and affiliations — is reachable without a mouse. Screen peruser testing is additionally basic, as it ensures that clients with visual impediments can explore and figure out your substance. Devices like NVDA (for Windows) and VoiceOver (for macOS) allow you to encounter your site according to the point of view of a screen peruser client, perceiving expected openings in text portrayals, content stream, and ordinary levelheadedness.

Accessibility Plugins and Extensions for WordPress

WordPress offers several modules to help with straightforwardness. WP Straightforwardness is a versatile module that watches out for different responsiveness needs, for example, empowering skip joins, fixing contrast issues, and guaranteeing certifiable plan naming. This module works on a piece of the specific bits of making your site open without requiring progressed coding information. Another consistent module, UserWay, adds a flexible responsiveness contraption to your site, permitting clients to change settings like text size, partition, and line separating as exhibited by their propensities. These modules work to give a more careful encounter and attract guests to change straightforwardness highlights thinking about their requirements.

Color Contrast Checkers for Visual Accessibility

Collection contrast is fundamental for clients with low vision or mostly visual hindrance, as it guarantees the message is conceivable against its understanding. WebAIM's Grouping Qualification Checker is a confusing contraption that speedily ponders your collection decisions as opposed to WCAG principles. By testing the division among text and foundation tones, this contraption guarantees consistency and further creates clearness. Different devices, similar to Difference Degree and Variety Safeguarded, offer extra help for picking combination things up that meet straightforwardness necessities. Guaranteeing solid combination contrast is a crucial yet persuading method for working on the experience for clients with visual weaknesses.

Mobile Accessibility Testing

With the ascending in conservative examining, it's principal to guarantee that your site's availability highlights contact PDAs. Google's Dynamic Test is an endless contraption for concentrating on your site's flexible solace. This test features issues, for example, text perspectives that are unnecessarily little to attempt to consider analyzing, buttons set nonsensically near one another or parts that require level examining. By settling these issues, you guarantee your site is available to adaptable clients, making it more straightforward for all guests to draw in with your substance paying little notification to the contraption.

Feedback and Analytics for Ongoing Improvement

Responsiveness redesigns ought to be steady, and commitment from authentic clients can offer critical snippets of data. Google Appraisal gives lead information, assisting you with perceiving models or pages with high skip rates, which could show straightforwardness challenges. Besides, giving a serious data structure for openness issues licenses clients to report express checks they experience. By dependably assembling and taking a gander at this information, you can take persistent actions up to your site's straightforwardness, making a more complete encounter that meets the making necessities of your gathering.

Chapter 10: Maintaining, Scaling, and Updating Your Website

Importance of Regular Maintenance

Keeping a WordPress site moving along as organized needs standard assistance to guarantee security, worth, and equivalence with the most recent turns of events. Support integrates stimulating WordPress center records, modules, and subjects to their most recent varieties. Each update usually addresses weaknesses, adds new parts, and further creates comparability with different mechanical gatherings. Disregarding these updates can allow your site to be uncovered to security dangers and execution issues. Booking routine assist checks, something with liking one time every month guarantees your site stays utilitarian, secure, and streamlined for clients.

Scaling Your Website as Traffic Grows

As your site traffic makes, scaling becomes basic to help expand clients with fascinating without compromising execution. Begin by checking traffic models and asset use to comprehend when to scale. Moving to a more critical level working with a plan, similar to a Virtual Confidential Server (VPS) or a serious server, gives more assets and dependability to high-traffic protests. Executing taking care of a Substance Transport Affiliation (CDN) dissipates server load and further improves page load speed for clients all around the planet. Routinely investigating these variables permits your site to oversee improvement impeccably, offering a smooth encounter and paying little respect to guest volume.

Content and Design Updates to Stay Relevant

Regions that curve are those that stay tremendous in both substance and plan. Fortifying substance dependably with blog entries, news, or new show pages keeps clients related as well as assists with Website improvement. Fundamentally, resuscitating game plan parts considering an impelling course of action models can keep your site enamoring and current. Minor changes, for instance, changing designs or endeavoring different things with new variety plans, can have an epic effect. It's critical to survey plan congruity dependably, guaranteeing that the site reflects current guidelines and client propensities.

Monitoring Site Performance and Analytics

Following site execution and client lead through appraisal instruments like Google Assessment and Google Mission Control Center is fundamental to perceiving regions for headway. These devices give snippets of data into skip rates, page load times, and client experiences, permitting you to address expected counteractions or execution issues. Consistently reviewing these assessments stays mindful of the ideal client experience and gives you information-driven direction to site changes. It moreover permits you to see and conclude issues before they become risky, guaranteeing steady site reliability and execution.

Security Audits and Backup Protocols

Remaining mindful of site security is a constant cycle that combines standard studies and fanning out a fantastic help show. Security reviews assist you with perceiving expected deficiencies and impede unapproved access. Utilizing a security module like Wordfence or Sucuri can motorize checks for problematic turn of events, obsolete reports, or threatening code. In like manner, basic is a reliable help structure. Modernize strongholds and store duplicates in a got, offsite locale to guarantee fast recuperation in the event of information difficulty. By organizing security checks and keeping strongholds, you shield your site and its substance from information breaks and sensible recreation time.

Testing Compatibility with Plugins and Themes

Closeness testing is essential for a well-working site. Right when WordPress center revives are conveyed, or you add new modules, equivalence with existing modules and subjects might be impacted. Testing new developments or updates in an arranged climate before doing them on the live site decreases the bet of breaking handiness or plant parts. A straightening-out page reflects your site, permitting you to securely endeavor different things with strength. This proactive methodology assists you with staying away from unforeseen issues and guarantees that all pieces of your site work strongly after restores.

Documentation and Standard Operating Procedures (SOPs)

As your site makes, making documentation and SOPs for routine undertakings can improve upkeep, particularly on the off chance that you hope to consolidate a social occasion. Recording procedures for attempts like resuscitating substances, coordinating modules, or watching out for security issues gives clearness and consistency. This documentation is especially critical in tolerating your use of extra accomplices or specialist undertakings, as it guarantees that your principles are stayed aware of. SOPs smooth out cycles and make it more straightforward to remain mindful of your site actually, even as it scales and advances.

10.1 Regular Maintenance Tasks and Backups

Importance of Regular Maintenance Tasks

Normal upkeep supports a safeguarded, stable, and high-performing WordPress site. The major objective is to guarantee that your site stays secure, sensible, and improved for clients. Upkeep undertakings like resuscitating WordPress center records, modules, and subjects safeguard the site from security inadequacies and comparability issues. WordPress reliably conveys resuscitates, keeping your site's current endpoints in the chance of being related to old programming. Performing standard upkeep reduces the probability of site individual time, as it allows you to decide possible issues before they influence accommodation.

Updating WordPress Core, Plugins, and Themes

Restores are pivotal for security and similarity, as they contain patches for deficiencies and bugs. WordPress center revives routinely remember refreshes for handiness, speed, and security. Essentially, modules and subjects get stimulated by creators to remain mindful of comparability with the most recent WordPress design and work on their elements. Checking for and applying empowers bit by bit keeps your site moving along exactly as expected. It's ideal to play out these reports on a straightening-out site page first to guarantee that they won't cause clashes with various modules or customizations on your live website page.

Conducting Security Scans and Malware Checks

Keeping a shielded WordPress site requires common security breadths to perceive malware or problematic exercises. Security modules like Wordfence or Sucuri can assist with computerizing these outcomes, checking for weaknesses, for example, old modules or compromised code. By seeing and facing any challenges early, you safeguard your site from information breaks, ruination, and other unsafe assaults. Standard outcomes ought to be organized over countless weeks, with expedient resulting practices expecting chances to be seen. As well as isolating, connecting with firewall insurance, and doing two-factor affirmation (2FA) add additional layers of safety.

Database Optimization for Improved Performance

A befuddled enlightening record can restrain your site for quite a while. Regular information base movement abstains from pointless information like spam remarks, post amendments, and destroyed things, which can in any case gather and increment the enlightening record's size. Instruments, for example, WP-Further develop work on this cooperation through motorizing information base cleanup and overhaul errands. Standard streamlining manages your site's speed and capacity, lessening load times and making a smoother client experience. Month-to-month enlightening file improvement holds your site page's show inside proper limits, especially for content-huge areas.

Backup Protocols: Setting and Testing Backup Solutions

Strongholds are a key piece of site upkeep, giving a security net if there should be an occasion of information lack, hacking, or different issues. Executing areas of strength for a strategy that makes and stores strongholds dependably is critical. Generally working with suppliers offers robotized support choices, yet utilizing a help module like UpdraftPlus or BackupBuddy gives you more control. In a perfect world, plan regular or countless weeks of fortresses and keep duplicates put away both on the spot and off-site (e.g., in spread limit). It's relatively essential to test support recuperation in some cases to guarantee that the help records are usable if fundamental.

Managing Broken Links and Redirects

Broken joins ruin client experience as well as affect Web smoothing out. Dependably checking for and fixing broken joins guarantees that guests are worked with to the right pages, forestalling frustration and updating your site's authenticity. Modules like Broken Affiliation Checker robotize this cycle by perceiving dead affiliations, which you can then supplant or clear out. Doing diverts for pages that have been erased or moved additionally assists clients and web with looking devices with finding the right assets. Tending to broken joins dependably keeps a consistent client experience and jam Site plan improvement regard.

Setting a Schedule for Maintenance Tasks

Fanning out an upkeep plan awards you to deal with these undertakings competently and try not to allow issues to gather. Detaching tries into ordinary, bit-by-bit, and month-to-month classes guarantees all parts of help get through without overpowering you. For example, strongholds and security breadths can be held bit by bit, while instructive assortment streamlining, module restores, and broken interface checks may be done month to month. Having a reliable arrangement besides guarantees that if you delegate these undertakings or get accomplices, everybody follows equivalent schedules for consistency and mindfulness.

10.2 Updating Themes, Plugins, and WordPress Core Safely

Importance of Updating WordPress Components

Standard updates to WordPress subjects, modules, and focus records are key for staying aware of safety, ampleness, and execution. These updates as regularly as possible direction fixes for shortcomings that, at whatever point left unpatched, could open your site to malware, developers, or similarity issues. Coterminous security invigorates and ceaselessly combines new parts, bug fixes, and execution refreshes, all of which add to an overwhelming client experience. Constantly reestablishing your page parts keeps it agreed with the latest business rules and advances, which is particularly huge in 2025, as WordPress and web improvement plans grow quickly.

Preparing a Backup Before Making Updates

A full-scale help of your site is central before any essential update. Updates can every so often achieve terrifying similarity issues or bumbles, and having assistance grants you to restore your site in case anything ends up being horrible. Modules like UpdraftPlus or

BackupBuddy can robotize the assistance cycle and store copies in the cloud. Make the two informative arrangements and report forts to ensure that each substance, setting, and plan is gotten. By helping with expanding your site, you limit the bet of losing data and can recover quickly from specific troubles during braces.

Using a Staging Environment for Testing

A fixing environment is an emulation of your live site that licenses you to test sustains without impacting your clients. This step is especially fundamental if you have a muddled site with different modules or customizations, as even little updates can impel comparability issues. Many websites offer a solitary tick sorting out plans, allowing you to clone your page and perform revives in a protected environment. In the organizing environment, you can evaluate whether the updates are working, perceive any customary discussions, and assess issues preceding pushing changes to your live site.

Updating WordPress Core

Reinforcing the WordPress focus should be rotated around, as it now and again as possible will overall huge security inadequacies and present new solace. WordPress lets you know in the dashboard whenever another transformation is open, and with a couple of snaps, you can present it. Enabling auto-vives for fundamental developments can ensure your site generally has the latest neighborhood without manual intervention. While quickening the middle, give close thought to any vehicle notes or cautions that go with the update, as these may outfit encounters into potential similarity issues with express subjects or modules.

Safely Updating Plugins

Modules increment the worth of your site, yet they can equivalently present security bets if old. To revive modules safely, start by inspecting the update notes given by the module fashioner, as these notes habitually notice any goliath changes or known issues. Strengthening modules uninhibitedly is overall around safer than mass reestablishing, as it licenses you to see and take a gander at issues if one express module causes an issue. If a module update is principal for security, spin around it whether it's held between your standard upkeep invigorates, as security should continually begin things out.

Updating Themes Without Losing Customizations

Reestablishing subjects is key for execution, likeness, and security, yet updates can overwrite customizations. If you've made changes to your subject records, consider making a youngster subject for your customizations. A youngster subject honors you to hold your customizations while reviving the parent point. Review the subject update notes for any colossal changes, especially to design documents. A few subjects give modified reestablishes, but it's wise to engage really when huge changes are realized to ensure no astonishing changes impact your site's appearance or handiness.

Testing and Monitoring the Site After Updates

Right when you've reestablished your WordPress parts, completely test your site to certify that everything is working exactly as expected. Check for visual changes, ensure instinctive parts (like plans and sliders) work, and test crushing pages for broken affiliations or show issues. Site solace can commonly be influenced by reestablishes, so playing out these checks holds any edge time or botches back from influencing client experience. Seeing instruments like Google Evaluation or a site-checking module can make you mindful of any post-update execution issues, ensuring that your site stays improved and supportive after reestablishes.

10.3 Tips for Scaling and Growing Your Site

Analyzing Your Current Site Performance and Growth Potential

Running before scaling your WordPress site, it's hard to concentrate on its nonstop show and perceive regions where updates are huge. Concentrate on assessments, for example, page load time, skip rate, and client commitment to comprehend how clients collaborate with your site. Instruments like Google Assessment, Google Search Control concentration, and execution modules can offer experiences into high-traffic pages, common social event length, and change rates. Understanding these assessments sees the pages or elements driving new development and those that could anticipate that refinement should help future adaptability and updated clients with experience.

Upgrading to a More Powerful Hosting Solution

A fundamental issue in scaling your site is working with climate. Imparted attempting to might be reasonable for little complaints yet miss the imprint on assets and execution expected for development. As your site draws in additional guests, think about moving to a Virtual Mystery Server (VPS), serious server, or oversaw WordPress working with plan, which offers more liberal assets and execution. Regulated WordPress working with, expressly, is improved for WordPress-unequivocal execution, giving quicker trouble times, more essential security, and serious help, which are fundamental as your traffic makes.

Optimizing for Speed and Responsiveness

Scaling a site requires an accentuation on speed and responsiveness, particularly as traffic increments. Begin by squeezing pictures, utilizing a substance development affiliation (CDN) to serve content speedier across land locales, and doing holding modules. Lazy stacking can diminish beginning page load times by stacking pictures when they show up. Taking out futile modules and redesigning your code —, for example, minifying CSS, JavaScript, and HTML — besides further makes speed. Google's Center Web Vitals are key execution markers that can impact web search instrument rankings and are essential for adaptability.

Leveraging Content and SEO for Increased Reach

As you scale, spin around creating substance and refining Site progression techniques to draw in new guests. Consistently scatter unparalleled grade, material substance that lines up with your gathering's advantages. Utilize long-tail watchwords and web page upgrade best practices to guarantee your substance positions well on web crawlers, and smooth out meta imprints, depictions, and picture alt text to help recognizable quality. Scaling your substance methodology may also consolidate exploring different streets concerning various media plans, similar to accounts or mechanized communications, and taking into account a substance schedule to remain mindful of trustworthy updates that keep your gathering going.

Building a Scalable Structure and Site Navigation

A making site requests an adaptable arrangement, which incorporates clear, coordinated course and content solicitation. While putting together site improvement, contemplate how extra pages, classes, or things will work within your continuous arrangement. An examined intelligent request — utilizing classes, names, and menus — is fundamental for both client experience and Web synthesis improvement. Guarantee that your site's basic course stays fundamental and instinctual, and use the breadcrumb course to assist clients with truly ending up inside the site. Scaling content without a firm improvement can induce a confounded encounter, so plan site connection contemplating future new development.

Implementing Advanced User Engagement Strategies

As traffic makes, draw in clients with systems, for example, email showing, altered content, and savvy highlights. Offer lead magnets, as electronic books or free starters, to make a partner base. Coordinate adjusted thoughts, live talk support, and appointed animate buttons to also encourage client obligation and drive changes. Finishing a client relationship the pioneers (CRM) framework that headings with WordPress can smooth out email showing and client obligation, permitting you to follow joint endeavors and target clients thinking about their way to deal with acting, as such upgrading adaptability through irregular obligation.

Scaling E-commerce Capabilities with WooCommerce Extensions

On the off chance that you work an electronic business page, WooCommerce outfits an adaptable stage with different expansions to help improve. Increments for cutting-edge thing separating, dynamic evaluating, deserted truck recuperation, and client care can assist with encouraging the shopping experience and expansion changes as your store scales. Furthermore, utilizing stock association extensions to facilitate with your providers guarantees you can oversee more prominent sales volumes profitably. Updating WooCommerce execution by utilizing a quick server, streamlining thing pictures, and arranging saving can in this way guarantee that your site handles the lengthy traffic without compromising pace or handiness.

Monitoring Site Health and Preparing for Future Growth

To help progression, interminable site seeing is critical. Use contraptions like Google Evaluation, uptime truly taking a gander at associations, and execution modules to follow key assessments and perceive expected issues before they influence client experience. Spread out a common study intended to check for broken joins, obsolete modules, and execution slacks. Also, remain informed about moving toward WordPress updates or security shows, as these can influence your flexibility plans. Planning for development requires remaining proactive, expecting likely difficulties, and executing resuscitates subject to the circumstance to guarantee your site is dependably prepared to oversee expanded requests.

10.4 Future-Proofing Your Website: Preparing for 2026 and Beyond

Anticipating Trends and Adapting to Evolving Technology

Future-fixing your WordPress site suggests staying flexible to changes in advancement and site arrangement designs. As the high-level scene rapidly creates, it's fundamental for screen designs in man-made cognizance, PC-produced reality, and extended reality that are affecting site helpfulness and client responsibility. By keeping a heartbeat on the latest movements, you can set up your website for revives that could integrate planning PC-based knowledge-controlled chatbots, further developing client experience with striking substance, or improving for additional created web record estimations. Making courses of action for potential overhauls today ensures that your site stays huge and serious later on.

Building a Flexible and Scalable Site Architecture

A versatile plan enables your WordPress site to easily oblige changes. Base on arranging a deliberate development that can be broadened or reconfigured as your site creates. For instance, using page designers like Elementor or Divi allows you to add and change content blocks without enormous code changes. Figure out your substance with an ideal, reliable plan that can be created, and make a good attempt to code parts that may be trying to change later. This approach gives you the flexibility to change your site as you present new things, groupings, or media types.

Staying Updated with WordPress Core, Themes, and Plugins

Regularly reviving your WordPress focus, themes, and modules is dire for security, convenience, and comparability. As new variations of WordPress are conveyed, they habitually consolidate security patches, incorporating updates, and similitude overhauls. Using a managed WordPress working with a provider that subsequently invigorates your middle records can chip away at this cooperation. In like manner, pick good modules and subjects with dynamic progression bunches that as frequently as conceivable conveyance revives. Ensuring likeness among your site's parts lessens the bet of broken features and guarantees that your site will run true to form as you change into the following couple of years.

Preparing for Enhanced Mobile and Voice Search Capabilities

With the continued climb of flexible scrutinizing and voice search, propelling your site for these functionalities is key. Responsive arrangement is as of now not optional; it's a requirement for staying aware of responsibility across devices. Go past fundamental convenient responsiveness by testing your site on various screen gauges and ensuring fast weight times on adaptable associations. Voice request headway incorporates using conversational watchwords and executing planning markup, which helps web search devices better sort out your substance. Focusing on these points of view can chip away at your site's presentation as compact and voice search become logically transcendent in client lead.

Implementing Security Protocols to Protect User Data

As organization wellbeing perils become more intricate, it is crucial to defend client data. Doing state-of-the-art security shows, such as SSL announcements, two-factor checks, and modified fortifications, is key for getting your WordPress site eventually. Reliably inspect your site for shortcomings and use firewalls or security modules to screen likely risks. If you handle sensitive data or money-related trades, consider embracing gauges like PCI consistency and GDPR rules. Protecting client data isn't just a best practice — it's principal for staying aware of client trust and ensuring that your site stays secure and real.

Optimizing for Core Web Vitals and User Experience Metrics

Google's emphasis on Center Web Vitals has made execution estimations fundamental for Web streamlining and client experience. These estimations — focused on stacking rate, instinct, and visual strength — should end up being considerably more tremendous later on. Further fostering your Middle Web Vitals can incite better rankings on web search devices and a redesigned client experience. Use execution improvement methods like lessening server response times, propelling pictures, and yielding offscreen content. Placing assets into client experience improvement as of now ensures your webpage stays merciless and is leaned toward using web crawlers as standards advance.

Building a Future-Ready Content Strategy

A plausible substance procedure incorporates making evergreen substances and expecting future group needs. Start by recognizing subjects that are unfading yet critical, allowing your substance to remain significant over an extended time. Separate your substance plans by including blog sections, accounts, infographics, and natural parts. This approach keeps clients associated across different media and engages bring visits back. Plan a substance plan that integrates conventional updates to existing posts and the extension of new material, making a predictable movement of new fulfilled that stays aware of Web composition upgrade rankings and keeps swarms associated as far as possible into what's to come.

Incorporating Scalability in Site Analytics and Data Collection

Strong data collection and assessment are key for scaling a future-arranged site. Unite assessment gadgets, similar to finding out about Examination and heatmaps, to procure encounters into client leads, traffic sources, and content execution. Set forth up genuine following to measure changes and gain custom reports to evaluate headway toward long-stretch objectives. With a solid examination foundation, you can change your methods as essential to agree with emerging examples and group tendencies. Using data-driven pieces of information, you can change your site to change client needs, promising it stays critical and effective as it creates.

Regularly Auditing Your Site for Continuous Improvement

A future-proof site isn't static; one is created through standard surveys and updates. Lead comprehensive audits on a semiannual reason to study execution, check for broken interfaces, and recognize old substances. Screen your site's security status, ensure consistency with any new rules, and evaluate whether your arrangement lines up with current style and client suspicions. Typical surveys license you to make pretty much nothing, reasonable changes for a long time, ensuring your page stays present day without requiring huge overhauls and that it continues to perform in a perfect world as web rules advance.

Conclusion

As we've ventured through the fundamental parts of building a strong, high-performing WordPress site in 2025, today's certain that is computerized scene requires both imagination and vital preparation. WordPress has developed into a flexible stage fit for supporting sites of different kinds and sizes, from individual online journals to internet business forces to be reckoned with, and with its proceeded headways, the potential for making effective sites has never been more prominent. The abilities and experiences shrouded in this guide prepare you to completely use WordPress, involving it as an adaptable, unique device to accomplish your particular objectives — whether they be driving commitment, helping deals, or building a local area.

Dominating WordPress isn't tied in with making a one-time, static site; it's tied in with building a versatile, living computerized resource that develops and works on after some time. By following the practices spread out in this aide, you're well-headed to making a site that will stay up with the most recent plan patterns, specialized developments, and client assumptions. Every part has presented indispensable ideas — from fundamental modules to cutting-edge customization and content techniques — all intended to assist you with making a novel and enduring internet-based presence. Whether you're new to WordPress or an accomplished engineer, these basic abilities will assist you with remaining on the front line.

In 2025 and then, speed, security, client experience, and availability will keep on being principal, as will remain associated with developing Website optimization and advertising patterns. As your site draws in additional guests, becomes its substance base, or scales its contributions, recall that continuous enhancements will keep it energetic and significant. Routinely examining, refreshing, and tweaking your site will guarantee it keeps up with superior execution, conveys a delightful client experience, and lines up with your objectives.

At long last, recall that WordPress is important for an immense, strong local area that cultivates learning, cooperation, and development. If you at any point feel adhered to or propelled to have a go at a new thing, tap into the abundance of assets, discussions, and individual WordPress clients to track down arrangements and offer thoughts. Dominating WordPress isn't just about building a site but about fostering the abilities and information to adjust in a speedy computerized world.

By investing the effort, energy, and care required, you're putting yourself in a good position with a site that mirrors the best expectations of plan, usefulness, and execution. Here's to making WordPress sites that stand apart today as well as flourish into the indefinite future.

www.ingramcontent.com/pod-product-compliance
Lightning Source LLC
LaVergne TN
LVHW080115070326
832902LV00015B/2597